Smart Love

Your Digital Guide to Love and Connection

Dave Amos

Unlock Transformative AI-powered Strategies to Build Trust, Avoid Misunderstandings, and Create a Happier, Healthier Relationship

Contents

The Future of Relationships with Modern Tools

Introduction

I vividly recall that moment. It was a late Thursday evening when my wife and I returned from a date night we had planned weeks before. As we drove into the driveway, a simple observation quickly sparked a conversation that escalated into an argument. I thought it was a perfect way to spoil a lovely night. However, this turned out to be more than just a ruined evening. What began as a casual discussion rapidly morphed into a once-in-a-lifetime clash—where neither of us was ready to relent. It was clear this was more than an ordinary dispute; it was the culmination of unaddressed, sensitive topics finally bubbling to the surface, expressed in a volatile manner through our words. Tempers intensified, words became sharp as daggers, and emotions surged. In the midst of the chaos, I teetered on the verge of uttering something that, deep down, I recognized could change everything. Just one thoughtless comment, one impulsive remark, and the bond we had cultivated over seven years could be shattered.

So, I walked away.

It wasn't an act of courage. It was survival—pure and simple. I needed space, not only to cool down but also to figure out why things had escalated the way they did. The words of my MBA Negotiations Class professor from years ago echoed in my mind: 'When you enter a conversation with a win-lose mindset, you are already the loser— regardless of the outcome'

As I sat in the quiet of another room, the gravity of the situation began to sink in. How had we gotten here? What had triggered this outburst? And, most importantly, what could I have done differently?

I wanted answers, but more than that, I wanted clarity. I needed a mirror—not the kind that reflected back my appearance, but one that could show me the deeper truths: my flaws, my patterns, my blind spots. So, on a whim, I turned to something unconventional. I opened my laptop and typed my frustrations, questions, and reflections into an AI-powered chat tool.

What happened next changed everything.

A New Kind of Companion

At first, it felt strange. I know what you are thinking: 'Who turns to a piece of software to figure out their relationship?' But as I typed out my feelings and described the argument in detail, the tool responded with surprising clarity. It didn't judge, didn't interrupt, and didn't take sides. Instead, it asked thoughtful questions that made me reflect more deeply on my actions and my wife's perspective.

"Why do you think she reacted that way?"

"What part of this situation is within your control to change?"

"How could you express yourself differently next time to avoid misunderstanding?"

These weren't groundbreaking questions, but they were exactly what I needed in that moment. They broke through the fog of my emotions and helped me see the situation with fresh eyes. The answers weren't always easy to swallow. I had to confront the ways my tone, words, and assumptions had contributed to the conflict. But instead of spiraling into guilt or defensiveness, I felt empowered. For the first time, I could see a clear path forward—not just for resolving this argument but for becoming a better partner overall.

From Survival to Strategy

That evening marked the beginning of a transformation in my relationship. Over the next few weeks, I started using this AI tool not only to analyze past arguments but also to prepare for future conversations. Before approaching delicate topics, I would ask it to help me frame my thoughts more clearly. If I felt overwhelmed by my emotions, I would describe the situation and ask for suggestions on how to respond more effectively.

The results were astonishing. I began to notice subtle shifts in how my wife and I interacted. Arguments became less frequent and less intense. Misunderstandings that once lingered for days were resolved in hours. Trust, which had taken a hit during that fateful argument, began to rebuild itself brick by brick.

But what struck me most was how this new tool didn't just help me communicate better—it helped me understand myself better. It held up a mirror to my habits, assumptions, and triggers, showing me areas where I could grow. It became a kind of digital coach, nudging me toward greater self-awareness and emotional intelligence.

Why Relationships Are So Hard

Let's face it: relationships are messy. They are the collision of two unique individuals, each carrying their own baggage, fears, and expectations. No matter how much you love someone, there will be moments when misunderstandings arise, tempers flare, and your connection feels strained.

And in today's fast-paced, hyperconnected world, maintaining a strong relationship is harder than ever. We are bombarded with distractions, from endless notifications to the pressures of work and social media. It's easy to lose sight of what matters most: the person right in front of you.

On top of that, we are rarely taught how to build healthy, lasting relationships. Most of us stumble through trial and error, learning as we go. We pick up communication habits from our parents (not all of them good), mimic what we see in movies, or follow advice from well-meaning friends. But rarely do we stop to ask: *Am I doing this right?*

This is where a tool like ChatGPT—or any other reflective resource—can make a difference. It acts as a nonjudgmental companion, helping you navigate the complexities of human connection with greater clarity and intention.

The Promise of This Book

This book is not about replacing human connection with technology. It's about enhancing it. It's about using the tools at our disposal to bridge the gap between intention and impact, between what we mean to say and how it's received.

Over the next sections, I'll share the exact strategies that helped me transform my relationship—strategies you can use not only with your partner but also with your friends, family, and colleagues. These tools are practical, actionable, and backed by both research and real-life experience.

Here's what you can expect:

- **Self-Awareness:** Learn how to identify your emotional triggers, patterns, and blind spots with the help of thoughtful prompts and questions.
- **Communication Mastery:** Discover how to craft clear, empathetic messages that minimize misunderstandings and build trust.
- **Conflict Resolution:** Turn arguments into opportunities for growth by reframing situations and finding common ground.
- **Emotional Intelligence:** Deepen your understanding of yourself and others, strengthening your ability to connect on a meaningful level.
- **Trust and Transparency:** Rebuild and maintain trust by practicing consistency, honesty, and accountability.

Each section is designed to be both practical and reflective, offering exercises, anecdotes, and insights you can apply immediately. Whether you're in a romantic partnership, a close friendship, or a professional relationship, these principles can help you navigate challenges and deepen your connections.

The Bigger Picture

While this book focuses on personal relationships, the lessons go far beyond the individual. At its core, this is a guide to building bridges—between people, perspectives, and possibilities. In a world that often feels divided, the ability to communicate with empathy and understanding is more valuable than ever.

Technology, when used thoughtfully, can be a powerful ally in this journey. It's not a replacement for human connection, but a tool that can help us navigate its complexities with greater ease and grace. By embracing this potential, we can create relationships that are not only stronger but also smarter.

A Quick Word on Technology

I want to address a common concern right off the bat: Isn't relying on a tool like ChatGPT for relationship advice a bit... impersonal?

I get it. The idea of using technology to navigate something as intimate as love can feel strange at first. But think of it this way: When you're struggling to communicate, you might turn to a therapist, a trusted friend, or even a book like this one for guidance. ChatGPT is simply another resource—one that happens to be available 24/7, doesn't judge, and offers insights tailored to your unique situation.

The key is to use it as a *companion,* not a crutch. The goal is not to let technology take over your relationships but to use it as a tool for reflection and growth. When approached with intention, it can help you become a better communicator, a more empathetic partner, and a stronger individual.

An Invitation to Begin

If you're reading this, chances are you're looking to improve a relationship in your life. Maybe you want to communicate better with your partner, rebuild trust with a friend, or strengthen bonds with your family. Whatever your goal, I want you to know that it's possible—and that this book can help you achieve it.

The strategies I'll share are not quick fixes or gimmicks. They require effort, honesty, and a willingness to grow. But if you're willing to put in the work, the rewards are profound. You'll not only transform your relationships but also gain a deeper understanding of yourself and the people around you.

So, let's dive in. Let's explore how technology, when used thoughtfully, can enhance our ability to connect, communicate, and love. Let's discover what it means to build *Smart Love*.

Are you ready? Let's begin.

The Reflective Companion — Understanding Yourself

"Until you make the unconscious conscious, it will direct your life, and you will call it fate."

— Carl Jung

1

The Power of Introspection

I used to pride myself on being logical and level-headed, someone who could keep his emotions in check even during tense situations. But if you had asked me during a heated argument, "What are you feeling right now?" I wouldn't have been able to answer. Sure, I could identify the obvious emotions like anger or frustration, but the deeper layers—fear, insecurity, or even sadness—were harder to pinpoint.

And that's the problem. Emotions are slippery things. They don't come with labels neatly attached, and they rarely announce themselves clearly. Instead, they show up as tension in your shoulders, a clenched jaw, or an inexplicable urge to lash out. If you can't identify what you're feeling, how can you possibly manage it?

That's where tools like ChatGPT can make a surprising difference. One of the most transformative habits I developed during my journey was a daily emotional check-in. At first, it felt awkward. Sitting down at my computer and typing out, *"I feel off today, but I don't know why"* felt like sending a text to no one in particular. But what I got back was unexpectedly helpful:

"It sounds like you're feeling unsettled. Could it be related to something specific that happened today? Or maybe a general sense of unease?"

This simple prompt opened a floodgate. I started typing about my frustrations at work, my worries about an upcoming project, and even small irritations I hadn't realized were bothering me. The act of putting my feelings into words helped me organize the chaos in my mind. And the responses—neutral, nonjudgmental, and curious—encouraged me to dig deeper into my emotions.

Why Naming Your Emotions Matters

Research shows that labeling emotions reduces their intensity. Psychologist Matthew Lieberman coined the term "affect labeling" to describe how naming your feelings activates the brain's prefrontal cortex, the area responsible for rational thinking. This activation dampens the activity in the amygdala, the brain's emotional center, allowing you to regain control over your reactions.

When you use a virtual companion to help you name your emotions, you're not just identifying what's wrong—you're giving your brain the tools to process and regulate those feelings. Instead of being swept away by a wave of anger or anxiety, you can anchor yourself with clarity.

Practical Tip*: The next time you feel overwhelmed, try this: Open a chat tool or even a blank document and write, "I'm feeling..." followed by whatever comes to mind. If you're stuck, describe your physical sensations (tight chest, racing thoughts, etc.). Often, the act of describing leads you to the underlying emotion.*

A Neutral Sounding Board

One of the most surprising things I discovered while using a virtual companion was how effective it was as a sounding board. In the past, when I needed to process a difficult situation, I'd turn to a close friend or my spouse. While their advice was often helpful, it wasn't always neutral. Friends and loved ones bring their own biases, emotions, and histories into the conversation, which can sometimes cloud their judgment.

A virtual companion, on the other hand, has no ego, no agenda, and no emotional investment. It exists to listen, reflect, and prompt you to think more deeply. When I described an argument or a tough decision, it didn't interrupt or jump to conclusions. Instead, it asked questions like:

- *"What do you think your partner was feeling in that moment?"*
- *"How might this situation look from their perspective?"*
- *"What part of this outcome could you control?"*

These questions weren't groundbreaking, but they were the right questions at the right time. They forced me to slow down and consider perspectives I might have overlooked.

The Power of Reflective Questions

In her book *Change Your Questions, Change Your Life,* psychologist Marilee Adams explains the difference between "judger questions" and "learner questions." Judger questions—*"Why does this always happen to me?"* or *"What's wrong with them?"*—shut down curiosity and keep us stuck in blame or defensiveness. Learner questions—*"What can I learn from this?"* or *"What's a better way to approach this?"*—open the door to growth and problem-solving.

Virtual companions excel at learner questions because they are programmed to foster exploration and curiosity. They don't react emotionally or get defensive; they simply guide you toward deeper understanding.

A Story: Turning Frustration Into Understanding

I remember one evening when my wife and I had another disagreement. I felt dismissed during a conversation, and my initial reaction was to sulk. Instead of letting that frustration fester, I turned to my virtual sounding board.

I typed: *"Why does she always interrupt me when I'm trying to explain something?"*

The response was gentle but pointed: *"Could it be that she's trying to express urgency or excitement? What might her intention be in those moments?"*

That simple reframing shifted my perspective. Instead of assuming malice or disrespect, I began to see her interruptions as expressions of enthusiasm. The next time it happened, I was able to respond with humor instead of irritation, which diffused the tension entirely.

Practical Tip*: Use a reflective companion to reframe your assumptions. After describing a frustrating situation, ask questions like:*

- *"What might their intention have been?"*
- *"How could I approach this differently next time?"*

From Reactivity to Reflection

If you've ever said something in the heat of the moment that you later regretted, you're not alone. Reactivity is a natural human response, especially when we feel attacked, misunderstood, or overwhelmed. But reactivity rarely leads to productive outcomes. More often, it escalates conflict and leaves both parties feeling worse.

One of the greatest lessons I learned during my journey was the value of pausing. That split-second decision to step away from an argument, take a deep breath, and consult my virtual companion often made the difference between escalation and resolution.

Here's an example: During an argument about finances, my wife accused me of being irresponsible—a comment that hit a nerve. My initial reaction was to snap back with a sarcastic remark, but I caught myself. Instead, I walked away, opened my laptop, and typed out exactly what had just happened.

The response was eye-opening: *"It sounds like her comment triggered a defensive reaction in you. Why might that be? Is there a deeper fear or insecurity driving your response?"*

Those questions forced me to reflect. I realized that her comment had struck a chord because I already felt insecure about our finances. My defensiveness wasn't about what she said but what I believed about myself.

When I returned to the conversation, I was able to express this vulnerability instead of lashing out: *"I think I got defensive earlier because I'm already feeling stressed about money. Can we talk about ways to handle this together?"*

Her response? Compassion and understanding. The argument dissolved into a productive conversation about shared financial goals.

Why Reflection Is More Powerful Than Reaction

When you take the time to reflect before responding, you shift the focus from winning the argument to understanding the issue. You create space for empathy and collaboration, which are essential for resolving conflict.

Practical Tip: *The next time you feel triggered, try this three-step process:*

1. ***Pause and Breathe:*** *Walk away if necessary. Give yourself time to cool down.*
2. ***Reflect and Write:*** *Use a virtual tool to describe the situation and your feelings. Ask questions like:*
   - *"Why did this trigger me?"*
   - *"What do I really want to communicate?"*

3. ***Respond Thoughtfully:*** *Return to the conversation with clarity and intention.*

The Power of Introspection in Action

The practices in this chapter may seem simple, but they are incredibly powerful. By checking in with your emotions, seeking clarity through reflective questions, and pausing before reacting, you can transform the way you show up in your relationships.

Introspection is not about blaming yourself or dwelling on your flaws. It's about understanding yourself—your triggers, your patterns, and your values—so you can navigate relationships with greater wisdom and compassion.

Remember, the goal isn't perfection. You will still make mistakes, lose your temper, and say things you regret. But with these tools in your back pocket, you'll be better equipped to repair, learn, and grow.

In the next chapter, we'll explore how identifying patterns in your behavior can further deepen your self-awareness and set the stage for lasting change.

2

Identifying Patterns in Your Behavior

I started noticing a pattern a few months into using my virtual companion for emotional check-ins. Many of my frustrations stemmed from the same situations, whether with my wife, friends, or colleagues. Someone might dismiss one of my ideas, make a joke at my expense, or interrupt me mid-sentence, and I'd feel a sudden surge of defensiveness or irritation.

It wasn't until I started digging deeper with my conversational partner that I realized these weren't isolated incidents—they were recurring triggers. The virtual companion's ability to hold a mirror up to my emotions was invaluable. After describing an argument or conflict, it often responded with prompts like:

- *"Does this situation remind you of anything else you've experienced recently?"*
- *"Have you felt this way before in similar circumstances?"*

When I took the time to reflect, I realized that many of my triggers were rooted in a fear of being dismissed or undervalued. This wasn't just about the present—it was about unresolved feelings from my past.

Why Triggers Matter

Triggers are emotional reactions tied to past experiences. They are like invisible tripwires in your psyche—small, seemingly harmless events can activate them, unleashing a flood of emotions. By identifying your triggers, you can begin to disarm them.

Research supports this idea. Studies in emotional regulation show that identifying patterns in your emotional responses helps you predict and manage them more effectively. It's not about avoiding triggers entirely but instead understanding them so they don't control you.

How to Spot Your Triggers

One of the best ways to identify your triggers is by journaling after conflicts. Using a virtual companion adds another layer to this process. For example, after describing a heated exchange, I would ask:

- *"What emotions stood out to me in that moment?"*
- *"What situations tend to evoke similar feelings?"*
- *"What might these reactions be trying to tell me?"*

These questions helped me trace my reactions back to their source, allowing me to approach future situations with greater awareness and calm.

Practical Tip: *Keep a trigger journal for two weeks. After any conflict or strong emotional reaction, jot down the event, how you felt, and what might have triggered you. Use a conversational partner to prompt deeper reflection and uncover recurring patterns.*

Why You Act the Way You Do

One of the biggest "aha" moments in my introspection journey came when I stumbled upon the concept of attachment styles. Developed by psychologists John Bowlby and Mary Ainsworth, attachment theory explains how the bonds we form in childhood shape the way we relate to others in adulthood.

There are four primary attachment styles:

1. **Secure:** You feel comfortable with intimacy and trust.
2. **Anxious:** You crave closeness but fear abandonment.
3. **Avoidant:** You value independence and struggle with vulnerability.
4. **Fearful-Avoidant:** You desire connection but also fear it, often resulting in push-pull dynamics.

I learned that I leaned toward an avoidant style, which explained why I sometimes withdrew emotionally during conflicts. On the other hand, my wife leaned toward an anxious style, which meant she sought reassurance and closeness when things felt uncertain. This mismatch often fueled our arguments.

Discovering Your Attachment Style

I was skeptical when I first brought up this concept with my virtual companion. But its prompts helped me reflect on my behaviors and connect them to my attachment patterns. It asked questions like:

- *"How do you typically respond when someone gets emotionally close to you?"*
- *"What do you fear most in relationships—being abandoned or feeling smothered?"*
- *"Do you notice yourself withdrawing or overcompensating during conflicts?"*

These questions weren't easy to answer, but they forced me to confront behaviors I'd previously ignored or rationalized.

Understanding your attachment style is akin to finding the user manual for your relationship habits. It helps you recognize why you act the way you do and how your partner's style influences the dynamic. Once I understood my avoidant tendencies, I could consciously work to stay emotionally present during conflicts rather than retreating.

Practical Tip: *Use a virtual tool or take an online attachment style quiz to identify your tendencies. Then, explore how these tendencies might show up in your relationships. Ask reflective questions to uncover ways you can balance your strengths and weaknesses.*

Recognizing the Roots of Conflict

Growing up, I often heard phrases like, "Don't air your dirty laundry" or "Keep your feelings to yourself" from non-family members in my environment. My family was super loving, but emotions—especially negative ones—weren't openly discussed. As a result, I developed a habit of bottling up my feelings and avoiding conflict.

This conditioning followed me into adulthood, where it clashed with my wife's upbringing. She came from a family where debates were encouraged and emotions were freely expressed. To her, silence during an argument felt like avoidance. To me, raising my voice felt like a loss of control.

It wasn't until I started working with my virtual companion that I began to see how these cultural and personal conditioning patterns were driving our conflicts. When I described a recurring argument, it prompted me to reflect:

- *"What beliefs about conflict did you inherit from your upbringing?"*
- *"How might your partner's background shape their approach to disagreements?"*
- *"What assumptions are you bringing into this situation?"*

Conditioning in Conflict

Our responses to conflict are often shaped by the environments in which we grew up. Cultural norms, family dynamics, and past experiences create a blueprint for how we handle disagreements. The problem is that we rarely stop to question these blueprints. We assume our way is the "right" way, which leads to misunderstandings and frustration.

Recognizing these influences isn't about blaming your past—it's about understanding it. When you uncover the roots of your conflict patterns, you gain the power to rewrite them.

A Story: Bridging the Gap Between Two Worlds

One of the most eye-opening moments in my relationship came when I asked my wife about her family's approach to conflict. She described lively debates around the dinner table, where opinions flew freely and disagreements were seen as opportunities for growth. Suddenly, her approach made sense. She wasn't trying to provoke me—she was trying to connect in the only way she knew how.

Likewise, when I shared my own upbringing, she began to understand why I valued calm and quiet during disagreements. This mutual understanding didn't eliminate our conflicts overnight, but it helped us approach them with more empathy and less judgment.

Practical Tip: *Reflect on how your upbringing and cultural background influence your approach to conflict. Use a virtual companion to explore questions like:*

- *"What beliefs about relationships did I learn from my family?"*
- *"How do those beliefs shape my behavior today?"*
- *"What assumptions might my partner be bringing into this dynamic?"*

Connecting the Dots

Identifying patterns in your behavior is like solving a puzzle. Each piece—your triggers, attachment style, and conditioning—reveals a deeper layer of understanding about yourself and your relationships. The goal isn't to "fix" yourself or eliminate all conflict. It's to approach your interactions with greater awareness, curiosity, and compassion.

By spotting recurring triggers, you can anticipate and manage your emotional reactions. By understanding your attachment style, you can navigate intimacy and vulnerability with greater intention. And by uncovering the roots of your conflict patterns, you can rewrite the scripts that no longer serve you.

These insights are the foundation for a deeper connection—not only with others but also with yourself. In the next chapter, we'll explore how to turn this self-awareness into actionable growth, setting the stage for healthier and more fulfilling relationships.

3

Building Emotional

Intelligence

Empathy is often described as the cornerstone of emotional intelligence. But while most of us understand the concept—putting yourself in someone else's shoes—it's far harder to practice when emotions are high. In the heat of an argument, empathy can feel like a distant luxury, overshadowed by the need to defend your own perspective.

That's where role-playing with a neutral guide, such as a virtual companion, can transform how you approach conflict. One of the most powerful exercises I discovered during my introspection journey was asking the tool to simulate my partner's perspective.

Here's an example:

After a disagreement about dividing household chores, I typed out my frustration: *"She never appreciates how much I'm doing around here!"*

The virtual companion replied:

"Imagine your partner responding to this. How might she describe her perspective?"

This prompt shifted my focus. I paused and thought about how she might feel—overwhelmed by her responsibilities or possibly unaware of the specific contributions I was making. By simulating her perspective, I could step out of my defensive mindset and approach the situation with greater curiosity.

Role-playing isn't just an abstract exercise; it's rooted in neuroscience. Research by Dr. Tania Singer on empathy shows that when we imagine someone else's experience, our brain's mirror neurons activate, allowing us to "feel" their emotions. This process enhances understanding and reduces emotional reactivity.

By using a virtual tool to guide this practice, you create a safe space to explore your partner's thoughts and feelings without the pressure of an actual confrontation. This makes it easier to approach the real conversation with an open mind.

Practical Tip: *The next time you're in a conflict, ask a conversational companion to simulate your partner's perspective. Use prompts like:*

- *"If I were them, what might I be feeling right now?"*
- *"What underlying needs or fears could be driving their reaction?"*
- *"How can I respond in a way that acknowledges their perspective?"*

This simple exercise can help you replace judgment with understanding and defensiveness with connection.

Strengthening Self-Compassion

Empathy isn't just for others—it's something we owe ourselves as well. Yet, for many of us, self-compassion is much harder to practice. We are often our own harshest critics, replaying mistakes in our minds and berating ourselves for not being "better."

I learned this the hard way after a particularly tough argument with my wife. I'd said something thoughtless in a moment of frustration, and although we'd resolved the issue, I couldn't stop replaying the moment in my mind. *"Why do I always mess things up?"* I thought.

When I turned to my virtual companion, it offered an unexpected response: *"What would you say to a close friend if they were in your situation? Could you offer yourself the same kindness?"*

This question hit me like a lightning bolt. Of course, I wouldn't speak to a friend the way I was speaking to myself. I would reassure them, remind them of their good intentions, and encourage them to learn from the experience without dwelling on it. So why was I denying myself that same grace?

Self-compassion is not about letting yourself off the hook or ignoring your mistakes. It's about recognizing that imperfection is part of being human and that growth comes from kindness, not self-criticism. Dr. Kristin Neff, a leading researcher on self-compassion, identifies three key components:

1. **Self-Kindness:** Treating yourself with the same care you'd offer a friend.
2. **Common Humanity:** Recognizing that everyone makes mistakes.
3. **Mindfulness:** Observing your emotions without judgment.

By reframing your inner narrative, you create a foundation for resilience and emotional growth.

Using Supportive Guidance to Reframe Your Narrative

A virtual tool can be a surprisingly effective ally in strengthening self-compassion. After describing a situation where I felt I'd fallen short, I'd ask for perspective:

- *"How can I reframe this experience in a positive way?"*
- *"What strengths did I show, even if the outcome wasn't perfect?"*
- *"What can I learn from this without being overly critical?"*

The responses often mirrored the kind of encouragement I'd offer someone else, helping me rewrite my inner dialogue with kindness and understanding.

Practical Tip: *The next time you catch yourself in a cycle of self-criticism, pause and imagine what you'd say to a friend in your shoes. If you're struggling, use a conversational companion to guide you through the process of reframing your narrative with compassion.*

Transforming Self-Awareness into Growth

Self-awareness is the foundation of emotional intelligence, but awareness alone isn't enough. To create meaningful change, you need to turn insights into action. This is where many of us get stuck. We recognize our patterns and identify areas for improvement, but we don't know how to take the next step.

During my own journey, I realized that my self-awareness often stayed in my head. I'd notice my triggers or understand my partner's perspective, but I didn't always translate those insights into actionable changes. That's when I began using my virtual companion to bridge the gap.

After reflecting on a conflict or behavior pattern, I'd ask the tool for specific, practical steps I could take to address the issue. For example:

When I noticed that I often interrupted my wife during conversations, I asked: *"How can I work on becoming a better listener?"*

The response included actionable suggestions like:

- *"Set an intention to pause for three seconds before responding."*
- *"Practice paraphrasing what your partner says to ensure you understand."*
- *"Limit distractions during conversations to stay fully present."*

These concrete steps gave me a roadmap for growth, turning self-awareness into tangible improvement.

Why Goals Matter

Setting actionable goals is a proven way to create lasting change. According to research in behavioral psychology, specific, measurable goals are far more effective than vague intentions. By breaking down your insights into manageable steps, you create momentum and build confidence in your ability to grow.

Practical Tip: *After each self-reflection session, identify one actionable goal based on your insights. Use the SMART framework (Specific, Measurable, Achievable, Relevant, Time-bound) to ensure your goal is clear and attainable.*

For example:

- *Instead of saying, "I'll try to be more patient," say, "I'll practice deep breathing before responding during our next discussion."*

Building Emotional Intelligence in Action

Practicing empathy, strengthening self-compassion, and turning self-awareness into growth are not isolated skills—they are interconnected. Together, they form the foundation of emotional intelligence, allowing you to navigate relationships with greater understanding, resilience, and intention.

When you practice empathy, you deepen your connection with others by seeing the world through their eyes. When you cultivate self-compassion, you strengthen your ability to recover from setbacks and approach growth with kindness. And when you turn self-awareness into action, you create tangible change that benefits both you and the people around you.

These practices aren't just theoretical—they're tools you can use daily to build stronger, healthier relationships. The key is to start small. Begin with one exercise—role-playing your partner's perspective, rewriting a critical inner thought, or setting a specific goal—and build from there.

In the next section, we'll explore how to use these skills to communicate more effectively, turning potential conflicts into opportunities for deeper connection. For now, take a moment to reflect on what you've learned. What insights have stood out to you? What small step can you take today to build your emotional intelligence?

Remember, growth is a journey, not a destination. Every step you take—no matter how small—brings you closer to the person and partner you want to be.

Talking It Out — Improving Communication

"Most people do not listen with the intent to understand; they listen with the intent to reply."

— Stephen R. Covey

4

Listening More, Talking Less

Listening is often misunderstood as the passive part of communication—a time when you sit quietly and wait for your turn to speak. But true listening is an active process. It requires focus, curiosity, and a genuine desire to understand the other person's perspective. It's also one of the hardest skills to master, especially when emotions are high.

For years, I thought I was a good listener. I nodded at the right times, maintained eye contact, and made an effort to remember details. But when I started using my virtual companion to analyze my communication habits, I realized how often I listened to respond rather than to understand.

One exercise that transformed my approach involved asking my virtual companion for feedback on how to listen better. Here's how it worked:

After describing a recent conversation, I'd ask: *"How could I have shown that I was truly listening?"*

The response might include insights like:

- *"Did you ask open-ended questions to encourage them to share more?"*
- *"Did you paraphrase what they said to confirm your understanding?"*
- *"Did you stay present, or were you distracted by your own thoughts?"*

These questions forced me to confront the ways I unintentionally derailed conversations—by jumping to conclusions, offering unsolicited advice, or letting my attention wander.

The Importance of Active Listening

Active listening isn't just about hearing words; it's about understanding meaning. Research from the Gottman Institute, a leading authority on relationships, shows that couples who practice active listening are better equipped to navigate conflict and build trust. The same principle applies to any relationship—when people feel heard, they feel valued.

Practical Tip: *Use a virtual communication coach to evaluate your listening skills. After any significant conversation, reflect on what went well and what could be improved. Ask questions like:*

- *"Did I give them space to express themselves fully?"*
- *"How did my responses show that I was paying attention?"*
- *"What cues might I have missed?"*

By treating listening as a skill to be refined, you'll gradually transform the way you connect with others.

Practicing Reflective Listening

Reflective listening is the art of paraphrasing what someone has said to confirm your understanding. It sounds simple, but it can feel awkward in practice—especially if you're not used to it. Early in my journey, I dismissed it as unnecessary. *"Why repeat what someone just said? Doesn't that sound robotic?"* I thought.

But I noticed something remarkable when I started experimenting with reflective listening, guided by my virtual companion. Conversations that previously felt tense or confusing suddenly became more collaborative. My wife, for example, would respond with phrases like, *"Yes, that's exactly what I meant,"* or *"No, not quite—let me explain it another way."*

This wasn't just about making her feel heard (though that was a big part of it). It was also about ensuring I truly understood her point before reacting.

How to Practice Reflective Listening

Using a conversational partner like ChatGPT is a low-pressure way to practice reflective listening. Here's an exercise I found particularly helpful:

1. **Describe a recent conversation where you felt misunderstood.**
   For example: *"I told my partner I was stressed about work, but they started giving me advice instead of listening."*
2. **Ask the tool to simulate the other person's response.**
   It might reply: *"You said you were stressed, but I wanted to help by offering solutions."*
3. **Practice paraphrasing the response.**
   Write: *"So what I hear you saying is that you were trying to be helpful, but I might have needed something different in that moment."*

The act of paraphrasing not only improves your listening skills but also helps you prepare for future conversations where reflective listening can defuse tension and build connection.

Practical Tip: *During your next conversation, try this simple framework:*

- *Listen fully without interrupting.*
- *Paraphrase what you heard: "It sounds like you're saying…" or "Let me make sure I understand…"*
- *Invite clarification: "Did I get that right?"*

Even if you don't get it perfect, the effort will show the other person that you care about understanding them.

The Pause Button Strategy

In the middle of a heated discussion, it's easy to let your emotions take over. You interrupt, raise your voice, or say things you don't mean—all because you're focused on winning the argument rather than resolving the issue. I've been guilty of this more times than I'd like to admit.

But one of the most effective tools I've learned to use is what I call the "Pause Button Strategy." This involves taking a deliberate pause—mentally and verbally—to regain composure before responding.

Here's how a virtual companion helped me practice this skill:

After describing an argument where I lost my temper, I asked for advice on how to stay calm in the future. The response suggested:

- *"Before responding, take a deep breath and count to three."*
- *"Ask yourself: What outcome am I hoping for in this conversation?"*
- *"If emotions feel overwhelming, suggest a brief timeout to gather your thoughts."*

These prompts became my go-to during real-life conflicts. Instead of reacting impulsively, I'd remind myself to pause, reflect, and respond thoughtfully.

The Science Behind Pausing

Pausing during a disagreement isn't just about buying time—it's about calming your nervous system. When you're triggered, your body enters fight-or-flight mode, flooding your brain with stress hormones that make rational thinking nearly impossible. Taking a few seconds to pause allows your brain to shift from a reactive state to a reflective one.

This practice is backed by research in emotional regulation. Dr. John Gottman's studies show that couples who take breaks during heated arguments are more likely to resolve conflicts constructively.

Practical Tip: *The next time you feel emotions rising during a conversation, try this three-step pause strategy:*

1. ***Physically Pause:*** *Take a slow, deep breath or a sip of water. If needed, step away briefly to collect your thoughts.*

2. ***Mentally Pause:*** *Ask yourself, "What's my goal in this conversation? What outcome am I hoping for?"*
3. ***Reengage Thoughtfully:*** *Return to the discussion with a response that aligns with your goal, rather than reacting out of frustration.*

Listening More, Talking Less in Action

Mastering the art of listening is one of the most transformative things you can do for your relationships. Whether you're using a virtual communication coach to refine your skills, practicing reflective listening to ensure understanding, or employing the Pause Button Strategy to stay calm during disagreements, these tools are designed to help you connect on a deeper level.

True listening isn't just about hearing words—it's about creating a space where the other person feels seen, heard, and valued. It's about prioritizing understanding over winning, connection over control.

In the next chapter, we'll dive into how to craft thoughtful responses that express your perspective and strengthen the bond you share with the people around you. For now, take a moment to reflect on your listening habits. Where are you strongest? Where could you improve?

Remember, listening is a skill that grows with practice and intention. Start small, and watch your relationships transform, one conversation at a time.

5

Crafting Thoughtful Responses

There's a unique kind of stress that comes with trying to craft the perfect message for a sensitive topic. Whether it's addressing a conflict with a partner, clarifying a misunderstanding with a friend, or delivering tough feedback at work, the stakes feel high, and the margin for error feels razor-thin.

In these moments, I often turned to my virtual companion as a drafting tool. One evening, after an argument with my wife, I wanted to apologize but also explain my perspective without reigniting the conflict. I typed out a draft:

"I'm sorry, but I feel like you overreacted, and I didn't mean what you think I meant."

Reading it back, I cringed. The tone was defensive, and it was clear I wasn't taking full accountability. So I asked my virtual companion for help:

"How can I rewrite this message to express my feelings without sounding defensive?"

The response reframed my words:
"I'm sorry for how I handled the situation earlier. I realize I could have been more thoughtful in how I communicated. Can we talk about what happened so I can better understand your perspective?"

This version struck the balance I was looking for—it conveyed remorse, avoided blame, and opened the door for a constructive conversation.

The Value of Drafting

Writing gives you the luxury of time—a chance to think through your words before they're spoken or sent. When you're dealing with sensitive topics, this extra step can make the difference between escalating a conflict and resolving it.

Practical Tip: *Use a drafting tool, like a conversational companion or even a blank document, to refine your message for sensitive situations. Ask for suggestions on tone, phrasing, or clarity to ensure your words convey exactly what you intend.*

Avoiding Misunderstandings

Have you ever said something with good intentions, only to have it land completely wrong? Misunderstandings like these are frustrating—and common—because tone and intent don't always align.

I remember one instance where I tried to reassure my wife during a stressful time by saying, *"Don't worry, it's not a big deal."* What I meant was, *"You're capable of handling this."* What she heard was, *"You're overreacting."*

It was a painful lesson in how tone and choice of words can create unintentional friction. To avoid similar situations in the future, I began using my virtual companion to preview my words before speaking.

Here's an example of how I'd test a message:

- I typed: *"Why didn't you finish that task?"*
- The tool suggested: *"Can we talk about what might have made it hard to finish the task?"*

The revised version softened the tone, removed the implied criticism, and encouraged collaboration instead of defensiveness.

How to Check Your Tone and Intent

Before entering a conversation or sending a message, pause to ask yourself:

1. *"How might the other person interpret these words?"*
2. *"Does this message reflect my true intention?"*
3. *"Am I making space for understanding, or am I being overly critical or dismissive?"*

By reviewing your tone and intent, you minimize the risk of miscommunication and build trust in your interactions.

Practical Tip: *Practice tone-checking by role-playing with a virtual tool. Share your intended message and ask for feedback on how it might be received. Adjust your phrasing until it aligns with your desired outcome.*

Saying What You Mean

One of the hardest parts of communication is expressing complex emotions in a way others can understand. When upset or overwhelmed, our words often come out jumbled, vague, or overly emotional. This confuses the listener and prevents them from fully addressing our needs.

A turning point in my communication was learning to convey my feelings using simple, clear language. Instead of saying, *"You always make me feel bad when I try to bring up issues,"* I learned to say, *"When you interrupt me, I feel dismissed, and it makes it harder for me to share my thoughts."*

This shift—from broad, accusatory statements to specific, descriptive ones—helped my wife and I understand each other better.

How to Simplify Complex Emotions

A virtual companion can act as a translator for your feelings, helping you turn abstract emotions into clear, actionable statements. Here's a step-by-step process I found helpful:

1. **Start with the Emotion:** Identify the primary feeling (e.g., frustration, hurt, disappointment).
2. **Describe the Trigger:** Specify what action or situation caused the emotion.
3. **State the Impact:** Explain how the trigger affected you.

For example:

- Original statement: *"You never listen to me!"*
- Revised version: *"When I feel interrupted, it makes me think my perspective isn't valued, and that's frustrating."*

The revised version avoids absolutes like "never," focuses on the specific behavior, and shares how it impacts you emotionally.

The Power of "I" Statements

Using "I" statements instead of "you" statements can also make a big difference. Statements like *"I feel hurt when..."* are less likely to provoke defensiveness than *"You make me feel..."* By taking ownership of your feelings, you invite collaboration rather than conflict.

Practical Tip: *Practice phrasing emotions simply by describing a recent experience to your virtual companion. Ask for feedback on how to make your message clearer or more constructive. Over time, this practice will help you communicate with greater confidence and precision.*

Crafting Thoughtful Responses in Action

Crafting thoughtful responses isn't about perfecting every word—it's about approaching communication with intention. Whether drafting a message for a sensitive topic, reviewing your tone to avoid misunderstandings, or finding the simplest way to express your emotions, the goal is to create clarity and connection.

When you take the time to think through your responses, you demonstrate respect for the other person and the relationship itself. You show that their feelings matter, that you value understanding and that you're willing to put in the effort to communicate effectively.

In the next chapter, we'll explore how to navigate disagreements and keep communication productive, even when emotions are high. For now, reflect on a recent conversation where your words didn't land as you intended. How could you have framed your message differently?

Remember, thoughtful communication is a skill you build with practice. The more intentional you are about your responses, the stronger and more meaningful your connections will become.

6

Non-Verbal Communication Matters

It's often said that communication is more than just words, and nowhere is this more evident than in body language. A raised eyebrow, a crossed arm, or even a shift in posture can speak volumes about how someone feels—sometimes more honestly than their words. Yet, most of us are so focused on what's being said that we miss the unspoken messages.

I experienced this firsthand during a conversation with my wife about a weekend plan. She said she was fine with my suggestion, but her arms were crossed, her gaze fixed on her phone, and her tone unusually flat. In the past, I might have taken her words at face value and moved on. But because I'd been working on recognizing body language, I paused and asked, *"Are you sure? You don't seem completely on board."*

Her response surprised me: *"Actually, I'd rather do something else, but I didn't want to disappoint you."*

By paying attention to her non-verbal cues, I was able to uncover what she really felt and avoid a potential misunderstanding.

Research by psychologist Dr. Albert Mehrabian found that in certain situations, up to 93% of communication is non-verbal. While this percentage varies depending on the context, it underscores the importance of paying attention to gestures, facial expressions, and tone. Body language reveals emotions that words might conceal, either intentionally or unintentionally.

Tips for Interpreting Body Language

- **Posture:** Notice how someone's posture changes during a conversation. Are they leaning in (engaged) or pulling back (defensive or disengaged)?

- **Gestures:** Watch for repetitive movements like tapping fingers (anxiety) or exaggerated gestures (excitement).
- **Eye Contact:** Shifting eye contact might indicate discomfort, while steady eye contact usually signals confidence or interest.
- **Tone and Pace:** Changes in tone or speaking speed often reflect shifts in emotion, even if the words remain neutral.

Practical Tip: During your next conversation, observe one aspect of the other person's body language. Reflect on how it aligns—or doesn't align—with their words.

Decoding Subtle Expressions

Sometimes, the most important messages are the ones that flash across someone's face for a split second. These fleeting emotions, known as micro-expressions, are involuntary and can reveal what a person is truly feeling before they have time to mask it.

I first noticed the power of micro-expressions during a discussion about finances with my wife. When I suggested a tighter budget, she smiled and nodded, but for a brief moment, I caught a flicker of tension—a furrowed brow, a tight jaw. Instead of moving on, I asked, *"You seemed hesitant when I brought this up. Is there something that worries you about the plan?"*

Her response confirmed my observation: *"I'm worried it might feel too restrictive, and we won't stick to it."* By acknowledging that fleeting moment of discomfort, we were able to address her concerns and find a solution that worked for both of us.

Dr. Paul Ekman, a pioneer in the study of emotions and facial expressions, identified seven universal emotions—anger, fear, sadness, disgust, surprise, happiness, and contempt—that are expressed similarly across all cultures. Micro-expressions of these emotions can appear in as little as 1/25th of a second, making them easy to miss if you're not paying attention.

How to Spot and Interpret Micro-Expressions

- **Look for Sudden Changes:** Watch for brief shifts in facial tension, such as a furrowed brow, flared nostrils, or a slight curl of the lip.
- **Focus on the Eyes:** The eyes often reveal emotions more clearly than other parts of the face. Look for narrowing (discomfort or anger) or widening (surprise or fear).
- **Practice Observing Neutral Faces:** Spend time observing people in casual settings to identify subtle emotional shifts.

Practical Tip: *Use reflective listening to address what you notice. For example, if someone's face momentarily shows sadness, you might say, "You seemed upset for a moment—am I reading that right?" Even if they downplay it, the effort shows you're paying attention.*

Bridging the Verbal-Nonverbal Gap

One of the greatest pitfalls in communication is misalignment between what we say and how we say it. A classic example is responding with "I'm fine" in a clipped tone while glaring at the other person. The words say one thing, but the tone and body language tell a completely different story.

This disconnect can erode trust and create confusion in relationships. During one particularly tense argument with my wife, I insisted I wasn't angry, even as I crossed my arms and avoided eye contact. Unsurprisingly, she didn't believe me. *"Your words are saying one thing, but everything else is saying something else,"* she pointed out.

Her comment hit me like a ton of bricks. I realized how important it is to align verbal and non-verbal communication. Saying the right words isn't enough—your tone, gestures, and expressions need to reinforce your message for it to be believable.

When your verbal and non-verbal communication are aligned, you come across as authentic and trustworthy.

Authenticity fosters connection because it shows the other person that you're being honest and transparent.

Conversely, misalignment—whether intentional or unintentional—can make others feel uneasy or doubtful. They may not consciously identify why, but they'll sense that something feels "off."

Practical Strategies for Alignment

1. **Be Mindful of Your Tone:** Match your tone to the message you're delivering. For example, if you're apologizing, your tone should convey sincerity and regret.
2. **Pay Attention to Your Body Language:** Ensure your gestures and posture support your words. An open stance with uncrossed arms signals approachability, while crossed arms or a rigid posture can create distance.
3. **Practice with Feedback:** Role-play a conversation with a trusted friend or virtual companion. Ask for feedback on whether your tone, words, and body language are consistent.

A Story: Finding Alignment in Tough Conversations

I remember a difficult conversation with a close friend where I needed to express disappointment about a missed commitment. I started by saying, *"I'm not upset—it's not a big deal."* But my tone was tight, and I avoided eye contact. He immediately became defensive, and the conversation derailed.

When I revisited the moment later with my virtual companion, it suggested a different approach: *"Try acknowledging your disappointment directly while maintaining a calm and understanding tone."*

The next time we spoke, I said: *"I was disappointed when we missed the deadline, but I know things have been hectic for you. Can we figure out a better way to handle this next time?"* The difference in his reaction was night and day. He felt respected and understood, and we were able to move forward productively.

Practical Tip: *Practice aligning your verbal and non-verbal communication during everyday interactions. Start small, like matching a warm smile to a casual "thank you," and build from there. Over time, this alignment will become second nature.*

Non-Verbal Communication in Action

Recognizing and mastering non-verbal communication is like learning a new language—one that enhances your ability to connect and communicate with those around you. Paying attention to body language, decoding subtle expressions, and aligning your words with your actions creates a richer and more authentic connection with others.

Non-verbal communication is always happening, whether you're conscious of it or not. The key is to make it intentional. You build trust and deepen relationships when your gestures, tone, and expressions reinforce your words.

In the next section, we'll explore how to navigate conflict with grace and transform disagreements into opportunities for growth. For now, take a moment to reflect on your non-verbal habits. What messages might you be sending without realizing it? How can you align your verbal and non-verbal communication for greater authenticity?

Remember, communication isn't just about what you say—it's about how you say it. And sometimes, the most meaningful messages are the ones you don't say at all.

Navigating Conflict with a Clear Mind

"A moment of patience in a moment of anger can prevent a thousand moments of regret."

— Chinese Proverb

7

Cooling Off Productively

It was one of those arguments where neither my wife nor I could let go. Every time one of us tried to "win" a point, the other fired back with a counterargument, escalating the tension. Finally, I said something sharp that I immediately regretted. She stormed out of the room, and I was left sitting there, the weight of my words settling like a stone in my chest.

In the past, I might have doubled down, replaying the argument in my head and mentally crafting my next comeback. But this time, I tried something different. I called a timeout—not just to stop the argument but to gather my thoughts and emotions.

I opened my laptop and turned to my virtual companion. I typed out the entire argument, raw and unfiltered, venting my frustration and confusion. The tool responded: *"It sounds like emotions were running high. What are the key points that mattered to you most in this discussion? Can you identify what might have mattered most to your partner?"*

That question shifted my perspective. Instead of fixating on the heat of the moment, I began to think more clearly about what the argument was really about. By the time we reconvened, I was able to apologize sincerely and approach the conversation with a calmer, more constructive mindset.

The Timeout Technique

The timeout technique is a powerful tool for de-escalating conflict. Neuroscience shows that during heated arguments, the brain's amygdala (responsible for emotional reactions) often overrides the prefrontal cortex (responsible for rational thinking). Taking a break allows your brain to reset, shifting you from reactivity to reflection. The timeout technique is most effective when a brief pause will not suffice.

How to Take an Effective Timeout

1. **Announce the Timeout:** Calmly say, *"I need a few minutes to cool off and gather my thoughts. Let's revisit this soon."*

2. **Engage in a Reflective Activity:** Write down your thoughts, talk to a neutral party, or use a virtual tool to process your emotions.

3. **Set a Time to Reconnect:** Ensure your partner knows this isn't avoidance by agreeing to revisit the conversation after the break.

Practical Tip: Use a virtual companion to unpack the argument during a timeout. Ask questions like:

- *"What emotions am I feeling right now?"*
- *"What part of this situation is within my control?"*
- *"What can I do to approach this conversation more constructively?"*

Reframing Arguments Through Neutral Eyes

One of the biggest challenges in resolving conflicts is stepping out of your own perspective long enough to see the other person's. When emotions are high, it's easy to dig in, focusing solely on your own point of view and dismissing theirs as "wrong" or "unreasonable."

I remember an argument with my wife about how we spent our weekends. I wanted more downtime, while she wanted us to be more social. At the time, it felt like an impossible standoff—two completely opposing desires with no middle ground. But when I sat down with my virtual companion, it asked me to summarize both sides:

- **My side:** *"I need quiet weekends to recharge after a stressful workweek."*
- **Her side:** *"She values weekends as an opportunity to connect with friends and family."*

Seeing the two summaries side by side made it clear that neither of us was "wrong." We simply had different needs. From there, it was easier to brainstorm solutions that addressed both perspectives, like alternating between social weekends and quiet ones.

Summarizing both sides of an argument is a technique often used in mediation. It forces you to articulate the other person's perspective in a neutral, respectful way, which not only helps you understand their viewpoint but also diffuses tension.

Using a virtual tool to guide this process can make it even more effective. After describing your argument, ask the tool to summarize both perspectives. Its neutrality ensures that neither side feels misrepresented, creating a foundation for finding common ground.

Practical Tip: *After any disagreement, take a moment to write down both sides of the issue. Use a conversational companion to help refine the summaries and identify overlapping needs or values.*

Preemptive Conflict Mapping

Not all conflicts come out of nowhere. In many cases, patterns of disagreement repeat over time—whether it's about household responsibilities, spending habits, or differing expectations. Recognizing these patterns can help you address potential conflicts before they escalate.

I learned this lesson relatively late - during our fifth year of marriage - when arguments about finances kept cropping up. Instead of waiting for the next fight to happen, I decided to map out the issue. I used my virtual companion to brainstorm: *"What recurring conflicts do we have, and what are the underlying causes?"*

Here's what I discovered:

- **Trigger:** Disagreements often arose after one of us made an unplanned purchase.
- **Underlying cause:** I felt anxious about saving for the future, while my wife valued spontaneity and treating ourselves occasionally.
- **Solution:** We created a "fun fund" with a set amount each month for guilt-free spending, reducing the friction over financial decisions.

By identifying the recurring trigger and addressing it proactively, we were able to stop the conflict cycle before it started.

How to Map Conflicts Proactively

Conflict mapping is about identifying patterns and preparing for them in advance. Here's how to do it:

1. **Identify Recurring Conflicts:** Think about the topics you argue about most often.
2. **Analyze the Triggers:** Consider what sparks these disagreements and why.
3. **Create Preemptive Solutions:** Brainstorm ways to address the underlying issues before they escalate.

Practical Tip: *Using a virtual companion can help you map out conflicts. Ask questions such as:*

- *"What patterns do you notice in our arguments?"*
- *"What are the underlying needs driving each person's perspective?"*
- *"How can we create systems or agreements to prevent future disagreements?"*

Cooling Off Productively in Action

Navigating conflict isn't about avoiding disagreements altogether—it's about handling them in a way that strengthens your relationship rather than undermines it. By using the Timeout Technique, reframing arguments through neutral eyes, and mapping conflicts proactively, you can approach disagreements with clarity, empathy, and purpose.

In the next chapter, we'll explore how to repair relationships after a conflict, rebuilding trust and connection through thoughtful actions. For now, reflect on a recent disagreement. How might these strategies have helped you navigate it more effectively?

Remember, conflict is an opportunity for growth—not just as a partner or friend, but as an individual. By learning to cool off productively, you create space for understanding, resolution, and deeper connection.

8

Repairing After an Argument

The Art of Apologizing

A sincere apology is one of the most powerful tools for repairing a relationship after an argument. Yet, many of us stumble when it comes to saying, *"I'm sorry."* We either rush through it to avoid discomfort or add qualifiers that dilute its impact: *"I'm sorry, but you have to understand why I did that."*

I learned the importance of a meaningful apology during an argument with my wife. I had forgotten a commitment we'd made, and when she called me out on it, I got defensive. The argument spiraled until I finally muttered a half-hearted, *"Sorry, I was busy."* Unsurprisingly, it didn't resolve anything.

Later, I turned to my virtual companion for guidance, typing, *"How do I apologize in a way that feels genuine?"* The response was eye-opening: *"A meaningful apology acknowledges the specific action, takes responsibility for the impact, and expresses a genuine commitment to doing better."*

I revisited the conversation with this framework in mind:

- **Acknowledgement:** *"I'm sorry I forgot about our plans. I can see how that made you feel unimportant."*
- **Responsibility:** *"That was my mistake, and I shouldn't have let other tasks distract me."*
- **Commitment:** *"Next time, I'll set a reminder so this doesn't happen again."*

The difference was immediate. My wife felt heard and valued, and we were able to move forward without lingering resentment.

Psychologists agree that a heartfelt apology can restore trust and repair emotional wounds. By taking responsibility and showing empathy, you validate the other person's feelings and pave the way for reconciliation.

Practical Tip: *When apologizing, avoid "if" or "but" statements, which can undermine sincerity. For example, instead of saying, "I'm* *sorry if I upset you," say, "I'm sorry I upset you." Own your actions and their impact fully.*

Rebuilding Trust Through Reflection

Trust is the foundation of any relationship, and when it's shaken by an argument or mistake, repairing it requires more than just an apology. It requires intentional effort to rebuild what was lost.

After another argument, where I had promised to follow through on something but didn't, I asked my virtual companion: *"How can I rebuild trust after breaking a promise?"* Its response helped me outline clear steps:

1. **Acknowledge the Breach:** Be honest about what went wrong.
2. **Understand the Impact:** Ask how the breach affected the other person emotionally.
3. **Take Action:** Commit to specific behaviors that demonstrate reliability moving forward.

For example, after letting my wife down by failing to show up on time for an important event, I followed this process:

- I acknowledged the issue: *"I broke my promise to be there, and I know that hurt you."*
- I understood the impact: *"It made you feel like I didn't value your time or the event."*

- I took action: *"I've set reminders on my phone for the next event, so this doesn't happen again."*

By reflecting on what had caused the breach and making tangible changes, I demonstrated that I was serious about earning back her trust.

Rebuilding trust isn't about grand gestures—it's about small, consistent actions over time. Each time you follow through on a promise, acknowledge their feelings, or make an effort to connect, you're adding bricks to the foundation of trust.

Practical Tip: *After a breach of trust, ask yourself, "What specific actions can I take to show I'm committed to making things right?" Write them down and follow through consistently.*

Learning from Mistakes

Arguments and mistakes can feel like setbacks, but they're also opportunities for growth—if you take the time to reflect and learn from them. After a particularly heated argument, I began asking myself: *"What could I have done differently to prevent this?"* This question eventually evolved into what I now call a relationship "lesson plan."

Here's how it works:

1. **Identify the Trigger:** What sparked the argument or mistake?

2. **Analyze Your Role:** What actions, words, or assumptions contributed to the conflict?
3. **Set a New Intention:** What can you do differently next time to avoid a similar issue?

For example, after an argument about feeling unheard during conversations, I created a lesson plan:

- **Trigger:** Feeling interrupted when I shared my thoughts.
- **My Role:** Reacting with frustration instead of calmly expressing my feelings.
- **New Intention:** Practicing reflective listening and calmly stating, *"Can I finish my thought before we discuss?"*

By treating each conflict as a learning opportunity, I was able to make small but meaningful adjustments that strengthened our relationship over time.

Reflecting on mistakes isn't about dwelling on what went wrong—it's about understanding the patterns and dynamics that led to the issue so you can change them. Over time, this practice builds emotional intelligence and resilience, helping you navigate future conflicts with greater ease.

Practical Tip: *After each argument, set aside 10 minutes to create a relationship lesson plan. Write down the trigger, your role, and a* *new intention. Share your insights with your partner to foster mutual growth and understanding.*

Repairing After an Argument in Action

Repairing a relationship after an argument isn't just about saying the right words—it's about following through with meaningful actions. By mastering the art of apologizing, reflecting on what caused the conflict, and creating a plan for growth, you can turn even the most challenging moments into opportunities to strengthen your connection.

Arguments are inevitable in any relationship, but how you repair and learn from them determines the health and longevity of your bond. In the next chapter, we'll explore how to set boundaries and navigate conflict in a way that respects both your needs and your partner's.

For now, think about the last argument you had. What did you learn from it? How might you apply these strategies to repair and grow your relationship?

Remember, the true measure of a strong relationship isn't the absence of conflict—it's the ability to recover, rebuild, and grow together.

9

Setting Healthy Boundaries

Boundaries often get a bad rap, misunderstood as barriers that create distance in relationships. In reality, healthy boundaries are the opposite—they foster connection, trust, and respect. Boundaries communicate your needs and expectations while allowing others to do the same, creating a dynamic where both parties feel valued.

I first realized the importance of boundaries when I noticed myself feeling overwhelmed by my wife's tendency to vent about her workday as soon as I walked through the door. While I wanted to support her, I also needed a few minutes to decompress after my own long day. Without a boundary in place, resentment began to build.

Finally, I brought it up in a conversation:

"I love hearing about your day, but I feel like I need 15 minutes to unwind when I get home. Can we talk after that?"

To my surprise, she agreed immediately. Setting that small boundary didn't push us apart—it allowed me to show up as a better listener when we did talk.

Boundaries matter because they create clarity. They let you express your needs in a way that's constructive rather than reactive. Instead of bottling up frustration or lashing out, you create a framework for mutual respect and understanding.

Examples of Healthy Boundaries

- **Emotional Boundaries:** *"I can support you, but I need time to process my own feelings first."*
- **Time Boundaries:** *"I need 30 minutes of uninterrupted focus while I finish this task."*
- **Physical Boundaries:** *"I'm not comfortable with this, and I'd prefer we find another way to handle it."*

Practical Tip: *Reflect on moments in your relationships where you've felt drained, overwhelmed, or taken for granted. These are often signs that a boundary is needed*

Practicing Boundary Conversations

Bringing up boundaries can feel uncomfortable, especially if you're worried about how the other person will react. But clear communication is key to setting boundaries that stick. One way to build confidence is by practicing boundary conversations through role-playing.

When I first started setting boundaries, I searched for options to help me prepare but AI tools have made this easier. For example, I wanted to set a boundary about work emails with a colleague who often sent requests late at night. Here's how I used role-playing to refine my approach:

1. **Describe the Situation:** I typed: *"How do I tell a colleague to stop emailing me after hours without sounding rude?"*

2. **Draft the Conversation:** The tool helped me craft a response: *"I value our collaboration and want to give my best work. To do that, I need to unplug after 6 PM. Can we agree to handle non-urgent emails during work hours?"*

3. **Practice Responses:** I role-played potential reactions, from agreement (*"That makes sense!"*) to pushback (*"But I need quick responses!"*), and prepared calm, respectful replies.

Role-playing helps you anticipate challenges and refine your message, so you can deliver it with confidence. It also allows you to practice staying calm and empathetic, even if the other person reacts defensively.

Practical Tip: *Use a conversational companion or trusted friend to role-play boundary conversations. Focus on:*

- *Stating your needs clearly: "Here's what I need."*
- *Framing the boundary positively: "This will help us work together more effectively."*
- *Remaining calm: "I understand this might be inconvenient, but it's important for me."*

Reinforcing Boundaries with Compassion

Setting a boundary is one thing—enforcing it is another. People may test your limits, intentionally or unintentionally, and it's easy to feel guilty or second-guess yourself. But maintaining boundaries is essential for your well-being and the health of the relationship.

The key is to reinforce your boundaries with compassion. For example, when my colleague continued sending after-hours emails despite our conversation, I replied the next morning:

"Thanks for your message. I'll get to this today during work hours, as we discussed. Let me know if there's an urgent issue that needs immediate attention."

By staying firm yet understanding, I reinforced the boundary without escalating the situation. Over time, the late-night emails stopped.

Enforcing a boundary doesn't mean being rigid or dismissive. It's possible to stay firm while acknowledging the other person's perspective. This balance strengthens the relationship by showing that you respect both your own needs and theirs.

Strategies for Compassionate Reinforcement

1. **Restate the Boundary:** Calmly remind the person of the agreement.
   - Example: *"I understand this is important to you, but I still need my 30 minutes of focus before we talk."*
2. **Acknowledge Their Feelings:** Validate their perspective while holding your ground.
   - Example: *"I know this is frustrating, and I appreciate your patience as we figure this out."*
3. **Offer Alternatives:** Suggest solutions that respect both parties' needs.
   - Example: *"If this timing doesn't work for you, let's find another way to handle it."*

Practical Tip: When enforcing boundaries, use "and" instead of "but" to show empathy while staying firm. For example, *"I understand this is hard for you, and this boundary is important for me."*

Setting Healthy Boundaries in Action

Boundaries aren't walls—they're bridges that connect people in ways that are sustainable and respectful. By recognizing where boundaries are needed, practicing boundary conversations, and reinforcing them with compassion, you create a relationship dynamic that values mutual respect and understanding.

In the next section, we'll explore how to build trust and transparency, essential components for maintaining strong, healthy relationships. For now, take a moment to reflect on your own boundaries. Are there areas where you feel drained or overextended? How might setting a boundary improve your relationships and well-being?

Remember, setting boundaries isn't selfish—it's a way to protect your energy so you can show up as your best self for the people who matter most.

Building Trust and Transparency

"Trust is built in very small moments."

— Brené Brown

10

Recognizing Trust Breakers

Trust isn't usually lost in a single, dramatic moment. More often, it erodes slowly, chipped away by small behaviors and unspoken doubts. Sadly, many of us overlook the warning signs until the damage is already done.

I learned this lesson the hard way in a previous relationship. Over time, I started noticing little changes: my partner would avoid direct answers to simple questions or make vague excuses for canceled plans. While none of these actions seemed catastrophic on their own, they planted seeds of doubt. Instead of addressing these feelings head-on, I ignored them, convincing myself I was overreacting.

By the time we finally confronted the issue, the trust had eroded so much that the relationship couldn't recover.

Recognizing trust breakers early allows you to address them before they grow into bigger problems. These red flags might include:

- Inconsistent behavior (e.g., saying one thing but doing another).
- Avoidance of certain topics or deflection during conversations.
- A noticeable lack of follow-through on promises.

How to Identify Trust Breakers

One of the most effective ways to spot red flags is by asking thoughtful questions, both of yourself and the other person. For example:

- *"Are there situations where I feel hesitant to trust them fully? Why?"*
- *"What specific behaviors make me feel uneasy?"*
- *"Have I communicated my concerns, or am I avoiding the conversation?"*

Practical Tip: *Keep a journal to track moments when trust feels strained. Write down what happened, how you felt, and any patterns you notice over time. This helps you identify recurring issues and address them proactively.*

The Power of Transparency

One of the most effective ways to restore trust when it's been shaken is through transparency. But being open and honest can feel vulnerable, especially if you fear the other person's reaction. This is where role-playing conversations can help you prepare.

After a disagreement about money caused tension in my marriage, I realized we needed to have a candid conversation about our financial goals. I turned to my virtual companion to help me plan the discussion. Here's how it unfolded:

1. **Describe the Situation:** I typed, *"How do I talk to my wife about the fact that I feel stressed when she makes large purchases without consulting me?"*
2. **Draft the Conversation:** The tool helped me frame my concerns positively: *"I'd like us to be more aligned on financial decisions so we can feel secure about our future."*
3. **Practice Responses:** I role-played potential reactions, from agreement (*"I understand where you're coming from"*) to defensiveness (*"Why are you trying to control my spending?"*). Practicing these scenarios helped me stay calm and empathetic during the real conversation.

Transparency fosters trust by eliminating the guesswork. When both parties openly share their thoughts, feelings, and intentions, there's less room for misunderstandings or hidden doubts.

Practical Tip: *Use a conversational companion or trusted friend to role-play tough conversations. Focus on:*

- *Stating your concerns clearly: "I feel uneasy when…"*
- *Explaining the impact: "It makes me worry about…"*
- *Inviting collaboration: "How can we work on this together?"*

The Trust Audit

Trust, like any other aspect of a relationship, varies in strength across different areas. You might fully trust someone to support you emotionally but feel unsure about their reliability in practical matters. Conducting a "trust audit" helps you identify these variations and create actionable plans to strengthen weak areas.

After an argument with my wife about forgotten commitments, I decided to assess the areas where we excelled in trust and where we struggled. I listed key aspects of our relationship, such as:

- **Emotional Support:** Do we feel safe sharing our vulnerabilities?
- **Reliability:** Do we follow through on promises?
- **Communication:** Are we honest and transparent with each other?

For each area, I asked myself:

- *"On a scale of 1 to 10, how much trust do I feel in this area?"*
- *"What specific behaviors contribute to or detract from this trust?"*

Here's what I discovered:

- **Strength:** Emotional support was a 9/10 because we consistently showed up for each other during tough times.
- **Weakness:** Reliability was a 6/10 because forgotten commitments created frustration.

From there, we created an actionable plan:

- Set up shared calendar reminders for important dates and commitments.
- Check in weekly to discuss any pending tasks or responsibilities.

A trust audit provides clarity, helping you pinpoint specific areas for improvement rather than generalizing the relationship as "good" or "bad." By breaking trust into smaller components, you can address weaknesses without overshadowing strengths.

Practical Tip: *Conduct a trust audit for a key relationship in your life. Identify one area of strength to celebrate and one area of weakness to address. Collaborate with the other person to create an improvement plan.*

Recognizing Trust Breakers in Action

Trust is the foundation of any healthy relationship, but it requires constant care and attention. By spotting red flags early, fostering transparency through open conversations, and conducting trust audits, you can identify and address issues before they become insurmountable.

Trust isn't about perfection—it's about consistency and effort. When you prioritize trust-building behaviors, you strengthen the foundation of your relationship, making it more resilient to challenges.

In the next chapter, we'll explore how to practice consistency in your words and actions to build trust that lasts. For now, reflect on the state of trust in your key relationships. Are there areas where trust feels shaky? How might these strategies help you rebuild and strengthen those connections?

Remember, trust isn't something you have—it's something you build, one moment and one action at a time.

11

Practicing Consistency

Small Steps, Big Results

Trust isn't built in grand gestures; it's built in the small, everyday moments where your actions align with your words. A promise kept, a commitment honored, or a task followed through on without reminders—these small steps accumulate into a solid foundation of trust.

I learned this lesson during a period when my wife and I struggled with household responsibilities. I'd often say, *"I'll handle it later,"* only to forget or procrastinate. Over time, these small lapses eroded her confidence in my reliability. When I finally recognized the pattern, I realized I needed to rebuild trust by showing up consistently in small, tangible ways.

I started with a simple accountability system. Each morning, I'd write down three tasks I promised to complete that day, no matter how small. At the end of the day, I'd check in with myself: *"Did I follow through?"* When I did, I'd note how it strengthened her trust in me.

Consistency signals reliability. When you consistently deliver on your promises, even in small ways, you demonstrate that you're dependable. Research in behavioral psychology shows that predictable, positive actions create a sense of safety and trust in relationships.

Practical Tip: *Start small. Choose one area of your life where consistency is lacking—whether it's communicating regularly, being punctual, or completing tasks on time. Commit to improving in that area and track your progress.*

Maintaining Integrity

Consistency isn't just about keeping promises—it's about staying true to your values. When your actions reflect your intentions, people trust that what they see is what they get. But when there's a gap between your words and actions, trust erodes quickly.

I faced this challenge during a conversation with a close friend. I had always emphasized the importance of mutual respect in friendships, but when I was late to several of our meetups, my actions didn't reflect my values. She called me out, saying, *"You say respect matters, but being late makes me feel like my time isn't important."*

Her words stung, but she was right. If I genuinely valued respect, I needed to demonstrate it consistently—not just in my words, but in how I showed up. From then on, I made a conscious effort to align my behavior with my values, arriving on time and giving her my full attention during our meetups.

How to Stay Aligned

- **Clarify Your Values:** Reflect on what matters most to you in your relationships (e.g., honesty, respect, kindness).
- **Audit Your Actions:** Ask yourself, *"Are my actions aligned with these values? If not, what needs to change?"*
- **Create Reminders:** Use prompts or tools to help you stay mindful of your intentions. For example, set a calendar reminder for important commitments or write a post-it note with your guiding principles.

Practical Tip: *Periodically review your relationships and identify areas where your actions could better align with your values. Share your intentions with the other person to hold yourself accountable.*

Following Through

Few things are as damaging to trust as broken promises, even when they're small or unintentional. Each time you fail to follow through, it sends the message—whether consciously or not—that your words can't be relied upon. Conversely, every promise kept, no matter how minor, strengthens the foundation of trust.

I experienced this dynamic in my marriage when I promised to plan a special date night but forgot to follow through. My wife didn't bring it up right away, but her disappointment was palpable. When I finally acknowledged my mistake, she said, *"It's not about the date—it's about feeling like I can count on you."*

From that moment on, I made follow-through a priority. I started using tools like shared calendars and reminders to ensure I didn't miss commitments. For larger promises, I'd break them into smaller steps to make them more manageable.

Follow-through demonstrates respect, accountability, and reliability. When you consistently keep your promises, you reinforce the belief that you're someone who can be trusted.

Practical Strategies for Following Through

1. **Underpromise and Overdeliver:** Be realistic about what you can commit to, and aim to exceed expectations when possible.
2. **Use Tools for Accountability:** Leverage calendars, reminders, or to-do lists to stay on track with commitments.
3. **Acknowledge Shortcomings Quickly:** If you can't meet a commitment, let the other person know as soon as possible and offer a plan to make it right.

Practical Tip: After making a promise, ask yourself: "What specific steps do I need to take to keep this promise? What might get in the way, and how can I address it?"

Practicing Consistency in Action

Consistency is about more than doing the right thing once—it's about showing up repeatedly and reliably over time. Building consistency in small ways, staying aligned with your values, and following through on promises creates a relationship dynamic that fosters trust and mutual respect.

In the next chapter, we'll explore how to rebuild trust after it's been broken, focusing on strategies to repair and strengthen your bond. For now, take a moment to reflect on your own consistency. Are there areas where you could be more reliable? How might small, intentional steps improve your relationships?

Remember, trust isn't built overnight. It's earned through steady, deliberate effort—one promise, one action, and one step at a time.

12

Trusting Yourself First

Trust in others begins with trust in yourself. When you have self-confidence, you approach relationships with clarity, resilience, and a sense of inner security. Without it, you may find yourself seeking constant validation, overthinking every interaction, or hesitating to express your needs.

I struggled with self-confidence in my early relationships. I often second-guessed my decisions, worried about saying the "wrong" thing, and felt overly dependent on others' approval. This lack of self-trust affected my ability to build healthy, balanced relationships.

What helped me turn the tide were simple, intentional exercises to rebuild my confidence. One of the most impactful was keeping a "small wins" journal. Each evening, I'd jot down three things I did well that day, no matter how minor they seemed—anything from completing a task on time to having a productive conversation.

Over time, these small acknowledgments built a sense of competence and self-assurance. I began to trust my ability to handle challenges and navigate relationships with authenticity. Engaging in intentional confidence-building exercises will boost your self-confidence levels, positively impacting all your relationships.

Confidence-Building Exercises

1. **Small Wins Journal:** Write down three achievements each day, focusing on your efforts and growth.
2. **Daily Affirmations:** Start your morning with affirmations like, *"I am capable of handling difficult conversations"* or *"My needs are valid and worth expressing."*
3. **Set and Meet Micro-Goals:** Break larger tasks into small, achievable steps. Completing them builds momentum and reinforces your sense of capability.

Practical Tip: *Commit to one confidence-boosting exercise for 14 days. Track how it impacts your sense of self-trust and your interactions with others.*

Overcoming Past Hurt

Past experiences of betrayal or disappointment can leave scars that make it difficult to trust others—or even yourself. If you've been hurt in the past, it's natural to approach relationships with caution, but unhealed wounds can create barriers to building meaningful connections.

I remember a time when a close friend broke my trust by sharing something I'd told them in confidence. For months, I carried the hurt and bitterness, which seeped into my other relationships. I found myself doubting people's intentions and holding back emotionally, fearing a repeat of that betrayal.

It wasn't until I turned to guided journaling that I began to release the pain. Using prompts from my virtual companion, I explored the emotions I had suppressed:

- *"What did this betrayal teach me about myself and others?"*
- *"What do I need to let go of to move forward?"*
- *"How can I rebuild trust in small, manageable steps?"*

By confronting my feelings head-on, I gained clarity and perspective. I realized that while the betrayal had hurt, it didn't define my ability to trust or my worth as a friend.

Journaling Prompts for Healing

1. *"What specific moments from the past still impact how I approach relationships today?"*
2. *"What did I learn about my own boundaries and needs from those experiences?"*
3. *"What steps can I take to rebuild trust in myself and others?"*

Practical Tip: *Dedicate 15 minutes each week to guided journaling about past emotional wounds. Focus on understanding your feelings and identifying actionable steps for healing.*

Becoming a Trustworthy Partner

Trust isn't just something you seek from others—it's something you cultivate within yourself and project into your relationships. Becoming a trustworthy partner means embodying qualities like reliability, authenticity, and accountability.

In one of my past relationships, I noticed that my words didn't always match my actions. I'd agree to plans out of politeness, knowing I wasn't fully committed, or make promises I wasn't sure I could keep. Over time, this eroded my partner's trust in me—not because I was dishonest, but because I wasn't consistent.

In a previous relationship, I realized that my words often didn't align with my actions. I would agree to plans out of politeness, knowing I wasn't fully committed, or make promises I was uncertain I could fulfill. This inconsistency gradually undermined my partner's trust in me— not because I was dishonest, but because I was inconsistent.

To improve, I adopted a straightforward mantra: *"Say what you mean, and mean what you say."* Before committing to anything, I would take a moment to reflect and ask myself, *"Am I truly willing and able to follow through on this?"* If the answer was no, I chose to be honest about it upfront.

How to Embody Trustworthiness

1. **Be Honest About Your Limits:** If you can't commit to something, it's better to say so upfront than to overpromise and underdeliver.
2. **Follow Through Consistently:** Even small commitments, like showing up on time or responding to a message, reinforce your reliability.
3. **Admit Mistakes Quickly:** If you fall short, acknowledge it, apologize, and outline how you'll make it right.

Practical Tip: Practice self-reflection after each interaction. Ask yourself:

- *"Did I show up authentically?"*
- *"Did my actions align with my words?"*
- *"What could I improve next time?"*

Trusting Yourself First in Action

Trusting yourself is the foundation for trusting others and building strong, resilient relationships. You create a solid base from which trust can grow by boosting your self-confidence, healing past wounds, and embodying reliability.

Self-trust isn't about being perfect—it's about knowing that you can handle challenges with integrity and resilience. When you trust yourself, you radiate confidence and authenticity, encouraging others to trust you in return.

In the next section, we'll explore how to foster emotional support and connection, building a relationship that thrives through understanding and mutual care. For now, reflect on your relationship with yourself. Are there areas where self-doubt or past hurt hold you back? How might these strategies help you rebuild trust in yourself and others?

Remember, the strongest relationships start with a strong foundation of self-trust. When you believe in your own reliability and worth, you create space for deeper, more meaningful connections with those around you.

A Toolkit for Emotional Support

"You don't drown by falling in the water. You drown by staying there."

— Ed Cole

13

Managing Stress Together

Stress is an inevitable part of life, but how we handle it—individually and as a team—makes all the difference. In a healthy relationship, stress doesn't have to create distance; it can become an opportunity to strengthen your connection. By working together to navigate tough times, you not only manage the stress itself but also build trust, empathy, and resilience.

Stress often feels like a solitary burden. When deadlines loom, or life throws curveballs, it's easy to retreat into your own head, leaving your partner feeling shut out. My wife and I fell into this pattern early in our relationship. I'd bury myself in work when I was overwhelmed, and she'd busy herself with other tasks, creating an invisible wall between us.

It wasn't until one particularly stressful week—she was swamped with deadlines, and I was dealing with a family issue—that we realized we needed a different approach. Instead of handling our stress separately, we decided to tackle it as a team.

That week, we tried a simple shared activity: a 20-minute walk after dinner every evening. During these walks, we'd take turns talking about what was on our minds without interruptions or attempts to solve each other's problems. It wasn't a miracle cure for stress, but it created a sense of togetherness that made the challenges feel less overwhelming.

Research from the American Psychological Association shows that couples who engage in shared activities during stressful periods report lower stress levels and higher relationship satisfaction. Shared activities release oxytocin, a bonding hormone that helps counteract the effects of cortisol, the stress hormone.

Ideas for Shared Stress Relief

1. **Physical Activities:** Go for a walk, try a yoga session, or have a dance break in your living room. Movement helps reduce stress and boosts mood.

2. **Mindfulness Practices:** Practice deep breathing, meditate together, or take turns sharing things you're grateful for.
3. **Lighthearted Distractions:** Watch a funny movie, play a game, or cook a new recipe together to break the tension.

Practical Tip: *Set aside 15–30 minutes daily for a shared activity that helps you unwind. Make it a non-negotiable part of your routine during stressful periods.*

Recognizing Stress Signals Early

Stress doesn't usually appear out of nowhere—it builds gradually, with small warning signs that are easy to miss if you're not paying attention. For me, stress often started with subtle cues: a tightness in my shoulders, interrupted sleep, or an unusual irritability. But when I ignored these signs, they would snowball into full-blown burnout.

In one particularly hectic month, both my wife and I were overwhelmed, but neither of us recognized it in each other. I snapped at her over a minor inconvenience, and she withdrew emotionally, feeling unsupported. It wasn't until we sat down and reflected that we realized we'd both been ignoring our stress signals—and each other's.

Common Signs of Stress and Burnout

- **Physical Signs:** Headaches, muscle tension, fatigue, or changes in appetite.
- **Emotional Signs:** Irritability, anxiety, or feelings of being overwhelmed.
- **Behavioral Signs:** Avoidance of responsibilities, procrastination, or increased arguments.

The key to managing stress is recognizing it early. One strategy my wife and I adopted was creating a "stress check-in" system. Once a week, we'd ask each other:

- *"How are you really feeling?"*
- *"What's been the most stressful part of your week?"*
- *"Is there anything I can do to support you right now?"*

This simple practice helped us identify stress before it spiraled and allowed us to show up for each other meaningfully.

Practical Tip: Develop a habit of regular stress check-ins with your partner. These don't have to be formal—just a few intentional questions to gauge your feelings.

Creating a Stress Action Plan

Stress is inevitable, but being unprepared for it doesn't have to be. After several rocky periods in our relationship where stress led to unnecessary conflict, my wife and I decided to create a stress action plan. This wasn't a rigid schedule or set of rules—it was a flexible framework to help us navigate tough times together.

Here's how we built our plan:

1. **Identify Triggers Together:**
   We listed common stressors that tended to disrupt our lives, like work deadlines, financial worries, or family obligations.
2. **Discuss Coping Preferences:**
   I realized I coped best by stepping back to process my thoughts quietly, while my wife preferred talking things through. Understanding these differences helped us avoid miscommunication during stressful moments.
3. **Set Clear Roles and Expectations:**
   During busy weeks, we'd agree on who would handle certain responsibilities, like cooking or errands, to lighten each other's load.
4. **Include Non-Negotiables:**
   We prioritized small rituals, like a nightly check-in or a weekend coffee date, to stay connected no matter how hectic life became.

Having a plan removes uncertainty and reduces the likelihood of miscommunication. Instead of reacting to stress in the moment, you have a proactive strategy to fall back on, which fosters teamwork and resilience.

Practical Steps for Creating Your Stress Action Plan

1. ***Set Aside Time:*** *Schedule an hour to sit down with your partner and discuss how you'll handle stress as a team.*
2. ***Brainstorm Together:*** *Identify triggers, coping strategies, and support methods that work for both of you.*
3. ***Write It Down:*** *Document your plan so you can refer to it during challenging times.*

Managing Stress Together in Action

Stress doesn't have to be a wedge that drives you apart—it can be a challenge that brings you closer together. You can navigate tough times with greater ease and connection by engaging in shared stress-busting activities, recognizing stress signals early, and creating a proactive action plan.

In the next chapter, we'll explore how to handle emotional overwhelm and build resilience as a team. For now, think about your relationship's current approach to stress. Are there patterns or triggers you could address together? How might these strategies help you create a stronger, more supportive partnership?

Remember, managing stress isn't just about surviving—it's about thriving together. With the right tools and mindset, you can turn even the most stressful moments into opportunities for growth and connection.

14

Navigating Emotional Overwhelm

Emotional overwhelm is like a tidal wave. One moment, you're handling life's challenges with some semblance of control, and the next, you're submerged by stress, fear, or sadness. In relationships, this overwhelm can ripple outward, impacting how you communicate, support each other, and handle conflict. Learning to navigate these intense emotions—both individually and together—is key to maintaining a strong, supportive bond.

Processing Big Emotions

When emotions feel too big to handle, the instinct is often to suppress or ignore them. I learned this the hard way during a particularly stressful period at work. Deadlines were piling up, and I felt like I was constantly teetering on the edge of burnout. Instead of acknowledging my emotions, I pushed them aside and tried to power through. The result? A minor inconvenience—spilled coffee—triggered an emotional outburst that left me feeling embarrassed and drained.

That experience taught me the importance of processing emotions as they arise. Mindfulness became my go-to tool for this. It allowed me to pause, acknowledge my feelings, and sit with those emotions without judgment.

Mindfulness Exercises for Emotional Processing

1. **The Body Scan:**
   Close your eyes and take slow, deep breaths. Starting at the top of your head, mentally scan your body, noting any areas of tension or unease. This approach helps you connect with your physical sensations, which are often tied to emotions.
2. **Name It to Tame It:**
   Label the emotion you're experiencing—whether it's frustration, sadness, or anxiety. Studies show that

naming emotions reduces their intensity by engaging the rational parts of the brain.

3. **Five-Sense Grounding Exercise:**
   Using the 5-4-3-2-1 method, identify five things you see around you, four things you can touch around you, three things you hear, two things you can smell, and one thing you can taste. This technique anchors you in the present moment, making overwhelming emotions feel more manageable.

Practical Tip: Schedule a five-minute mindfulness break each day, especially during stressful times. Use it to check in with your emotions and process them in the moment.

Breaking Down the Overwhelm

When life feels overwhelming, it's often because we're trying to tackle everything at once. I remember when my wife and I were juggling too many commitments—work deadlines, family events, and household projects—all while trying to maintain some semblance of a social life. The sheer number of tasks left us paralyzed, snapping at each other over minor issues instead of working together.

One evening, we sat down and listed everything weighing on us. Seeing it all on paper felt overwhelming, but then we did something transformative: we started breaking it down.

Steps to Break Down Overwhelm

1. **Brain Dump Everything:** Write down every task, worry, or responsibility swirling in your mind. This clears mental clutter and gives you a concrete starting point.
2. **Prioritize:** Sort the list into categories: urgent, important but not urgent, and non-essential.
3. **Take One Small Step:** Choose one manageable task to tackle first. Completing even a tiny action can create momentum and make the bigger picture feel less daunting.

That night, we decided to focus on one urgent task: planning our upcoming family event. By addressing it together, we reduced our stress and strengthened our teamwork.

Practical Tip: Use the "two-minute rule" for small tasks: if it takes less than two minutes to complete, do it immediately. For larger tasks, break them into smaller steps and focus on one at a time.

Reframing Negativity

Life is full of setbacks, and it's easy to let them spiral into negativity. However, with practice, you can master the art of reframing challenges as opportunities for growth and connection. This shift isn't about ignoring difficulties but choosing a perspective that empowers you instead of holding you back.

One of the most powerful lessons I learned about reframing came during a particularly difficult argument with my wife. We had planned a weekend getaway, but a work emergency on my end forced us to cancel. I felt guilty, and she was understandably disappointed. Initially, we both focused on what we'd lost—the trip, the relaxation, the time together. But after cooling off, we decided to approach it differently.

Instead of lamenting the canceled trip, we reframed the situation:

- **Lesson Learned:** We realized the importance of setting boundaries with work to protect our personal time.
- **Opportunity Gained:** We used the weekend to tackle a home project we'd been postponing, turning it into a fun, bonding activity.

How to Reframe Negativity

1. **Ask Empowering Questions:** Instead of asking, *"Why does this keep happening to me?"* try asking, *"How can we develop from this situation?"* or *"What lessons can I take away from this?"*
2. **Find the Silver Lining:** Even in difficult situations, there's often a hidden benefit or

opportunity. Identify one positive aspect of the setback.

3. **Focus on Solutions:** Shift your energy from dwelling on the problem to brainstorming ways to address it.

Practical Tip: When you or your partner are feeling stuck in negativity, take a few moments to reflect together. Ask each other, "What's one small, positive takeaway we can find in this situation?"

Navigating Emotional Overwhelm in Action

Emotional overwhelm doesn't have to derail your relationship. You can navigate life's difficulties with grace and resilience by using mindfulness exercises to process big emotions, breaking down challenges into manageable steps, and reframing setbacks as opportunities.

In the next chapter, we'll explore how to practice daily gratitude and celebrate small wins, creating a foundation of positivity that sustains your relationship even in tough times. For now, think about a recent moment when you felt overwhelmed. How might these strategies have helped you manage the situation differently?

Remember, navigating emotional overwhelm is about progress, not perfection. Each small step strengthens your ability to face challenges together, creating a partnership that thrives through life's ups and downs.

15

Practicing Daily Gratitude

Gratitude is often described as the secret ingredient to a happy life, and its impact on relationships is equally profound. When you actively practice gratitude, you shift your focus from what's lacking to what's abundant, creating a mindset of appreciation and connection. In relationships, gratitude fosters positivity, deepens bonds, and acts as a buffer against challenges. It's not about grand gestures but acknowledging the everyday moments that make your relationship special.

The first time I kept a gratitude journal, I was skeptical. Life felt overwhelming, and the idea of writing down "three good things" each day seemed simplistic. But as I committed to the practice, I noticed a subtle shift. Instead of fixating on the stressful parts of my day, I began looking for moments of joy and connection—my wife's laugh during dinner, the way she made my favorite tea without me asking, or how we tackled a household project together.

Over time, the act of writing these moments down not only made me feel more positive but also deepened my appreciation for her. It reminded me of the many ways she enriched my life, even on the most challenging days.

Studies have shown that practicing gratitude enhances overall well-being, strengthens relationships, and even reduces symptoms of anxiety and depression. By focusing on positive moments, you train your brain to notice them more frequently, creating a cycle of positivity.

How to Start a Gratitude Journal

1. **Choose a Format:** Use a notebook, an app, or even a shared journal with your partner.
2. **Set a Time:** Dedicate five minutes each evening to reflect on your day.
3. **Be Specific:** Instead of vague entries like *"I'm grateful for my partner,"* write, *"I'm grateful for the way they encouraged me when I was feeling unsure today."*

Practical Tip: *If you're journaling solo, share one entry with your partner each week. If you're journaling together, use it as an* *opportunity to reflect on and celebrate each other's contributions to the relationship.*

Fostering a Culture of Appreciation

Gratitude doesn't have to be a private practice. In fact, sharing your appreciation with your partner is one of the simplest and most effective ways to strengthen your bond. Yet, many of us overlook this habit in the rush of daily life.

I realized this during a conversation with my wife, where she admitted feeling unappreciated for the little things she did, like keeping our home organized or managing family schedules. It wasn't that I didn't notice—I just didn't say it out loud. From that day on, I made a point to express my gratitude daily, whether it was a simple "thank you" or a more heartfelt acknowledgment.

Daily Prompts to Foster Gratitude

1. **Morning Check-In:** Start the day by asking, *"What are you looking forward to today?"* and acknowledge their response.
2. **Midday Reminder:** Send a quick message like, *"I appreciate how you handled [specific task]."*
3. **Evening Reflection:** Share one thing you're grateful for about your partner before going to bed.

Over time, these small expressions of gratitude create a culture of appreciation, where both partners feel valued and supported.

Practical Tip: *Use technology to your advantage. Set a daily reminder to express gratitude to your partner, ensuring this habit becomes part of your routine.*

Celebrating Small Wins Together

Life is filled with small victories—meeting a deadline, solving a problem, or just surviving a tough day. Celebrating these wins, however minor they may seem, can bring joy and accomplishment to your relationship.

My wife and I started this practice during a particularly challenging year. One evening, after finally fixing a leaky faucet that had been a source of frustration, we decided to celebrate by ordering takeout and watching our favorite show. It was a small gesture, but it turned a mundane accomplishment into a shared moment of happiness.

Acknowledging and celebrating small wins reinforces a sense of teamwork and positivity. It reminds you both that even during stressful times, there are reasons to smile and moments to cherish.

Ideas for Celebrating Together

1. **Mini Celebrations:** After completing a shared task, treat yourselves to a dessert, a short walk, or a toast to your accomplishment.
2. **Weekly Highlights:** At the end of each week, share one thing you're proud of and celebrate it together.
3. **Create Rituals:** Establish traditions for celebrating milestones, big or small, like lighting a candle, playing a favorite song, or writing each other a note.

Practical Tip: Keep a list of small celebration ideas for different occasions. When something worth celebrating happens, choose an activity from the list to mark the moment together.

Practicing Daily Gratitude in Action

Gratitude isn't just a feeling—it's a practice, a mindset, and a way of life. By journaling your positive moments, expressing daily appreciation, and celebrating small wins together, you create a relationship dynamic that thrives on acknowledgment and joy.

In the next section, we'll explore how to use these tools to navigate the future of relationships, blending gratitude and technology to build stronger, more connected partnerships. For now, reflect on how gratitude shows up in your relationship. Are there opportunities to express more appreciation or celebrate your wins together?

Remember, gratitude isn't about perfection. It's about finding and cherishing the good in every moment, no matter how small. With time and intention, this practice can transform your relationship into a source of constant joy and connection.

The Future of Relationships with Modern Tools

"The best way to predict the future is to create it."

— *Peter Drucker*

16

What Modern Tools Can Do for Relationships Today

In a world where technology influences every part of our lives, it's no surprise that it's also reshaping how we connect, communicate, and grow in our relationships. From apps that help us express our feelings to virtual tools that guide us through difficult conversations, modern technology is unlocking new possibilities for emotional connection and relational growth.

Let's explore how current tools are transforming relationships, from enhancing communication to revolutionizing therapy practices, through stories of real people who've successfully integrated technology into their relationships.

Exploring Current Tools

Communication is a major challenge in relationships. Misunderstandings, mismatched expectations, and unexpressed needs can all create tension. Modern tools, however, are making it easier than ever to bridge these gaps.

Take apps like **Paired**, designed specifically for couples. Paired offers daily prompts to spark meaningful conversations, quizzes to understand each other better, and exercises to improve communication skills. For my wife and me, one Paired prompt transformed how we talk about our day. It asked, *"What's one thing your partner did recently that you really appreciated?"* Her response about how much she valued my help with a home project sparked a conversation that deepened our mutual understanding and gratitude.

Another invaluable tool is **Reflectly**, a journaling app that encourages self-reflection and emotional awareness. While it's not specifically for couples, Reflectly helped me recognize patterns in my emotional reactions. By tracking my moods and reflecting on triggers, I could approach conversations with greater clarity and calmness.

How These Tools Help

- **Prompts and Exercises:** Apps like Paired provide structured ways to have conversations that might feel awkward to initiate on your own.
- **Self-Reflection:** Journaling apps like Reflectly promote self-awareness, which improves how you show up in your relationship.
- **Accountability:** Many tools offer reminders to practice communication exercises, helping you build consistency.

Practical Tip: Choose one communication-focused app and commit to using it for a month. Set a goal to complete at least one activity or prompt per day and reflect on how it impacts your relationship.

New Approaches to Therapy

Therapy has long been a powerful tool for improving relationships, but modern technology is making it more accessible and personalized than ever before. Apps like **BetterHelp** and **Talkspace** connect users with licensed therapists through text, audio, or video sessions, removing barriers like scheduling conflicts or geographic limitations.

A friend and his wife first explored therapy through an app after struggling to find a local therapist who fit their needs. Using BetterHelp, they were matched with a counselor who specialized in communication for couples. The flexibility amazed them: they could text the therapist throughout the week and schedule sessions around their busy schedules. This ease of access encouraged them to stay consistent, and within a few months, they noticed tangible improvements in how they navigated conflicts.

Technology is also bringing innovative formats to therapy. **ReGain**, for example, offers therapy designed specifically for couples, allowing both partners to engage with the same therapist through a shared virtual platform. Similarly, apps like **Lasting** provide therapy-inspired tools for self-guided relationship growth, from guided audio sessions to interactive exercises.

The Benefits of Tech-Driven Therapy

1. **Accessibility:** No more commuting or rearranging schedules—sessions are available anywhere.
2. **Consistency:** Regular check-ins through apps keep therapy top-of-mind, even between sessions.
3. **Customization:** Tools like Lasting allow you to focus on specific areas of your relationship, whether it's intimacy, communication, or trust.

The Rise of AI in Therapy

Emerging tools like AI-powered virtual companions are also playing a role. Platforms like **Woebot** use AI to provide evidence-based emotional support, offering strategies for managing stress and improving relationships. While not a replacement for traditional therapy, these tools can complement it, providing immediate guidance during emotionally charged moments.

Practical Tip: *If therapy feels intimidating, start with a self-guided app like Lasting. Explore its tools to address one specific area of your relationship and assess how it impacts your communication and connection.*

Stories of Success

The impact of technology on relationships isn't just theoretical—it's changing lives in tangible ways. Here are a few real-life stories that highlight how couples have used modern tools to grow closer:

Story 1: Rekindling Connection Through Conversation Prompts

When Sam and Mia, a couple married for 10 years, found themselves drifting apart, they turned to the app Paired. They began completing the app's daily prompts together, starting with lighthearted questions like, *"What's a memory that always makes you smile?"* Over time, the prompts became deeper, encouraging them to discuss their values, fears, and dreams. Within weeks, they noticed a renewed sense of closeness and understanding.

Lesson Learned: Structured tools like conversation prompts can help couples reconnect by creating opportunities for meaningful dialogue.

Story 2: Managing Conflict with AI-Powered Coaching

Taylor and Jordan, a couple in a long-distance relationship, struggled with recurring conflicts over communication. They started using Woebot to process their emotions individually before addressing tough topics together. By reflecting on Woebot's prompts, like *"What underlying need is driving your frustration?"* they were able to approach conversations with empathy instead of defensiveness.

Lesson Learned: AI-driven tools can help individuals manage their emotions, making tough conversations more productive.

Story 3: Overcoming Trust Issues with Virtual Therapy

After a breach of trust nearly ended their relationship, Priya and Arjun turned to ReGain, a couples therapy app. Their therapist guided them through exercises to rebuild trust, like sharing vulnerabilities and setting clear boundaries. The app's flexibility allowed them to engage in therapy consistently, even during Priya's business trips. Over time, they rebuilt their connection and developed a stronger foundation of trust.

Lesson Learned: Virtual therapy provides the guidance and structure couples need to navigate complex challenges, even with busy schedules.

Practical Tip: Use these stories as inspiration to explore tools that fit your unique needs. Whether it's improving communication, managing conflict, or rebuilding trust, there's a resource that can help.

What Modern Tools Can Do for Relationships Today in Action

Modern tools aren't just conveniences—they're powerful allies in building and sustaining healthy relationships. By exploring apps and resources for communication, leveraging technology-driven therapy options, and learning from the successes of others, you can harness the potential of these tools to strengthen your connection.

In the next chapter, we'll explore how to use technology responsibly, ensuring it enhances rather than hinders your relationship. For now, think about your own relationship. Are there areas where a modern tool could make a difference? How might these resources help you communicate more effectively, manage conflicts, or deepen your bond?

Remember, technology isn't a replacement for human connection—it's a tool to enhance it. By using these tools intentionally, you can build a relationship that thrives in today's fast-paced, tech-driven world.

17

Responsible Use of Technology in Relationships

As powerful as modern tools can be in enhancing relationships, they come with challenges. Technology, when used carelessly, can become a barrier rather than a bridge. Overreliance, privacy concerns, and an overemphasis on digital solutions can create distance instead of fostering intimacy. The key is in using these tools responsibly, ensuring they complement—rather than replace—the human connection at the heart of every relationship.

Avoiding Overreliance

It's easy to fall into the trap of leaning too heavily on technology. With apps offering prompts for every conversation and AI tools ready to guide emotional challenges, the convenience can make us forget that relationships thrive on raw, unfiltered human connection.

I experienced this firsthand when my wife and I started using a relationship app to improve communication. While the prompts were helpful, we found ourselves depending on them too much. If we didn't complete the daily exercises, we'd assume we weren't making progress, forgetting that simple acts like an unprompted hug or spontaneous conversation were equally important.

The turning point came when we decided to use the app as a supplement, not a crutch. We set boundaries, dedicating time for unstructured conversations and quality time without digital tools. This balance allowed us to enjoy the benefits of technology while keeping our relationship grounded in genuine connection.

How to Avoid Overreliance

1. **Set Clear Limits:** Decide how often you'll use relationship tools, balancing them with offline interactions.

2. **Prioritize Spontaneity:** Make room for organic moments of connection, like impromptu date nights or shared laughter.

3. **Reflect Regularly:** Ask each other, *"Are these tools enhancing or replacing our connection?"* Adjust accordingly.

Practical Tip: *Establish "tech-free zones" in your relationship, such as no devices during meals or evening conversations, to prioritize face-to-face connection.*

Privacy and Consent

As technology becomes more integrated into relationships, questions of privacy and consent become increasingly important. Many tools, from AI-driven apps to shared calendars and trackers, require access to personal information. While these features can enhance coordination and understanding, they also introduce risks if used without clear boundaries.

I once heard a story about a couple who used a shared location-tracking app to stay connected. Initially, it was a practical tool for coordinating plans. But over time, one partner began using it to monitor the other excessively, creating tension and eroding trust. The issue wasn't the tool itself—it was the lack of mutual consent and clear boundaries.

Guidelines for Privacy and Consent

1. **Discuss Boundaries Openly:** Before using a tool, have a candid conversation about what feels comfortable for both of you.
   - Example: *"Are we both okay with sharing our locations? If so, how will we use this feature respectfully?"*
2. **Review Data Policies:** Understand how apps handle your data and ensure both partners are comfortable with the level of sharing involved.
3. **Respect Autonomy:** Avoid using tools to monitor or control your partner. Trust is built on mutual respect, not surveillance.

Practical Tip: Revisit privacy settings and agreements regularly to ensure that they align with your comfort levels and relationship dynamics as they evolve.

Balancing Tech and Intimacy

While technology can enhance relationships, it's crucial to ensure it doesn't overshadow the personal, intimate moments that define true connection. This balance requires intentionality—integrating tools in a way that supports, rather than distracts from, your time together.

I remember a period when my wife and I became overly reliant on our shared calendar app. While it was great for managing logistics, it started feeling like our relationship was reduced to tasks and reminders. We decided to reclaim intimacy by adding "intentional time" to our calendar: weekly date nights, tech-free evenings, and even short, spontaneous outings.

By carving out space for connection that wasn't dictated by technology, we found ourselves laughing more, talking deeper, and enjoying each other's company in a way that no app could replicate.

Strategies for Balancing Tech and Intimacy

1. **Use Tools as Enhancers, Not Replacements:** Let technology streamline logistical tasks (like scheduling) so you can focus more on meaningful interactions.
2. **Create Rituals Without Tech:** Establish traditions that don't rely on digital tools, like a nightly check-in or a weekend hike.
3. **Monitor Tech Overlap:** Be mindful of how often your conversations or interactions revolve around tools, and redirect your focus when needed.

Practical Tip: Schedule a weekly "connection review" to reflect on how well your balance between tech and intimacy is working. Ask each other, "What worked well this week? What could we do differently?"

Responsible Use of Technology in Relationships in Action

Technology has the power to strengthen relationships, but only when used thoughtfully. By avoiding overreliance, respecting privacy and consent, and balancing tech with intimacy, you can harness its benefits without sacrificing the authenticity of your connection.

In the next chapter, we will look to the future and explore how emerging technologies, such as AI and virtual reality, are poised to transform relationships. For now, take a moment to reflect on your own use of technology in your relationship. Are there tools that enhance your connection? Are there areas where tech might be overshadowing intimacy?

Remember, technology is a tool—it's how you use it that determines whether it brings you closer or creates distance. With intentionality and care, you can ensure it supports the vibrant, human connection at the heart of your relationship.

18

Future-Proofing Your Love Life

The future of relationships is intertwined with technology. As tools evolve and integrate further into our daily lives, their role in how we connect, communicate, and grow together will only deepen. Yet, even as technology transforms our love lives, the essence of relationships—trust, empathy, and shared values—remains unchanged. Future-proofing your love life means leveraging technology wisely while staying grounded in the timeless principles that make relationships thrive.

Lifelong Companions

Imagine having a digital assistant that doesn't just remind you of anniversaries but helps you plan meaningful celebrations tailored to your partner's love language. Or a virtual relationship coach that tracks your communication patterns and suggests ways to resolve recurring conflicts. These scenarios aren't far-off dreams—they're becoming a reality as technology continues to evolve.

In my own relationship, tools like shared calendars and communication apps have already become indispensable. But the possibilities for the future are even more exciting. AI-powered platforms like **Lovewick and Official** are starting to offer daily relationship check-ins, tracking emotional trends over time to help couples spot patterns and address challenges proactively.

One couple I know shared how they used such a tool to strengthen their bond. After months of feeling disconnected due to busy schedules, they began using a relationship tracker to reflect on their daily emotions. Over time, they noticed a pattern: their happiest days were the ones where they spent even 15 minutes in intentional conversation. Armed with this insight, they prioritized evening chats, transforming their dynamic.

How Technology Strengthens Bonds

- **Proactive Support:** Tools can identify issues before they escalate, offering tailored advice for improvement.
- **Enhanced Connection:** Apps encourage couples to reflect and communicate, deepening understanding.
- **Personalization:** AI-driven insights can suggest activities or approaches unique to your relationship.

Practical Tip: Start exploring one advanced tool, like a relationship tracker or virtual assistant, and experiment with how it fits into your life. Treat it as an enhancement, not a replacement, for intentional connection.

Staying Grounded in Humanity

While technology offers incredible possibilities, it's essential to ensure it aligns with—and supports—your core values. The risk of relying too heavily on digital tools is losing the spontaneity, vulnerability, and raw emotion that make relationships human.

I once fell into this trap during a stressful time at work. Instead of having heartfelt conversations with my wife about how I was feeling, I relied on journaling apps and AI tools to process my emotions. While they provided clarity, I realized I wasn't sharing my struggles with her, which left her feeling shut out.

The lesson was clear: technology can guide self-reflection, but it can't replace the courage to share openly with your partner. Relationships thrive on the messy, imperfect moments that no app can replicate.

How to Stay Grounded in Humanity

1. **Prioritize Personal Connection:** Use tools to facilitate, not replace, human interaction.
2. **Reflect on Values:** Ask yourself, *"Does this tool align with what matters most in my relationship?"*
3. **Embrace Imperfection:** Don't let the pursuit of "optimization" overshadow the beauty of real, unfiltered moments.

Practical Tip: Create a "values checklist" for your relationship. When integrating a new tool, ensure it supports—not contradicts—your shared principles, such as honesty, empathy, or quality time.

Adapting to Change

As technology continues to evolve, so will the way we navigate relationships. Virtual reality date nights, AI relationship coaches, and even augmented reality tools to help long-distance couples feel more connected are on the horizon. Adapting to these changes requires openness to innovation while maintaining clarity about what matters most in your relationship.

For example, a friend of mine, June, recently shared how she and her long-distance partner used VR to bridge the miles between them. With headsets, they explored virtual museums, watched movies in simulated locations, and even shared "meals" in a simulated café. While this didn't replace physical closeness, it provided a creative way to stay connected during a challenging time.

At the same time, June emphasized the importance of balancing these innovations with simple, heartfelt gestures, like handwritten letters and spontaneous video calls. These analog touches kept their relationship rooted in authenticity, even as they embraced cutting-edge solutions.

How to Embrace Growth Responsibly

1. **Stay Curious:** Explore emerging tools with an open mind, but don't rush to adopt every new trend.
2. **Focus on Balance:** Pair digital solutions with analog practices that prioritize personal connection.
3. **Reevaluate Regularly:** Periodically assess whether your use of technology aligns with your evolving relationship goals.

Practical Tip: *When trying a new tool or innovation, set aside time to reflect on its* **impact**. *Ask: "Is this helping us grow closer? If not, what adjustments can we make?"*

Future-Proofing Your Love Life in Action

The future of relationships will undoubtedly be shaped by technology, but the heart of every partnership remains deeply human. By embracing lifelong companions in the form of evolving tools, staying grounded in your shared values, and adapting to change with intentionality, you can future-proof your love life for the challenges and opportunities ahead.

In the next section, we'll explore how to integrate these tools and strategies into your daily routine, creating a sustainable approach to building a strong, enduring relationship. For now, reflect on how you've already embraced technology in your relationship. Are there areas where it enhances your bond? Are there ways to stay more connected to what matters most?

Remember, the goal isn't to let technology lead your relationship but to let it support and amplify the connection you already share. With the right mindset, the future of love isn't just bright—it's limitless.

Conclusion

Love, like any meaningful endeavor, requires intention, effort, and a willingness to grow. As you've journeyed through this book, you've explored how to navigate relationships with a blend of timeless wisdom and modern tools. From mastering communication to managing stress, from building trust to future-proofing your connection, you've been equipped with strategies to foster a relationship that is both resilient and fulfilling.

This isn't the end of the journey—it's the beginning of a smarter, more intentional approach to love. In this conclusion, we'll reflect on the growth you've achieved, consolidate the strategies into a practical toolkit, and leave you with an invitation to thrive in your relationships.

Reflecting on Growth

At the heart of this book lies a simple truth: relationships flourish when you combine self-awareness, empathy, and intentional action. Let's revisit the key lessons and strategies that have guided you toward smarter love:

Understanding Yourself

- **Emotional Check-Ins:** Regularly label your emotions and process them with mindfulness or reflective tools to gain clarity and calm.
- **Identifying Patterns:** Recognize recurring triggers, attachment styles, and cultural conditioning to uncover the roots of conflict.
- **Building Emotional Intelligence:** Practice empathy, cultivate self-compassion, and transform self-awareness into actionable growth.

Improving Communication

- **Listening More, Talking Less:** Develop active and reflective listening skills to understand and connect deeply.
- **Crafting Thoughtful Responses:** Use drafting tools to refine your words, ensuring clarity and empathy.
- **Non-Verbal Communication:** Recognize and align body language, tone, and actions for authentic connection.

Navigating Conflict with Grace

- **Cooling Off Productively:** Use timeouts and neutral reflection to defuse heated moments.
- **Repairing After an Argument:** Offer meaningful apologies, rebuild trust, and learn from mistakes to grow stronger together.
- **Setting Healthy Boundaries:** Establish clear, compassionate boundaries to protect and nurture your relationship.

Building Trust and Transparency

- **Recognizing Trust Breakers:** Identify red flags and address them proactively.
- **Practicing Consistency:** Align your words and actions to demonstrate reliability.
- **Trusting Yourself First:** Build self-confidence and embody authenticity as a foundation for trust.

A Toolkit for Emotional Support

- **Managing Stress Together:** Share stress-busting activities, recognize warning signs, and create a stress action plan.
- **Navigating Emotional Overwhelm:** Process big emotions, break down challenges, and reframe setbacks constructively.
- **Practicing Daily Gratitude:** Celebrate small wins and nurture a culture of appreciation.

Embracing Modern Tools Responsibly

- **Enhancing Connection:** Use apps and technology to improve communication and emotional awareness.
- **Staying Grounded:** Balance technology with humanity, ensuring tools support your values.
- **Adapting to Change:** Embrace innovation while staying connected to what matters most.

These strategies aren't one-time fixes—they're lifelong practices. The more you integrate them into your daily life, the more they will transform your relationship.

Your Relationship Toolkit

To help you take action, here's a practical checklist of tools and strategies you can refer to as you continue your journey:

Self-Reflection and Emotional Awareness

- Keep a **journal** to track emotions, triggers, and patterns.
- Practice daily **mindfulness exercises** like body scans or grounding techniques.
- Use **conversation prompts** to explore deeper aspects of yourself and your partner.

Communication and Conflict Resolution

- Implement **active listening techniques**, such as paraphrasing or summarizing your partner's words.
- Draft sensitive messages or rehearse difficult conversations with a trusted friend or virtual tool.
- Take structured **timeouts** during conflicts to regain composure.

Building and Rebuilding Trust

- Conduct regular **trust audits** to assess areas of strength and weakness.
- Align your actions with your words by keeping a simple **commitment tracker**.
- Apologize meaningfully, acknowledging both your actions and their impact.

Stress Management and Emotional Support

- Create a **stress action plan** to navigate tough times as a team.
- Practice **gratitude journaling**, sharing one thing you appreciate about each other daily.
- Schedule **intentional time** for shared activities, like a weekly check-in or a fun outing.

Integrating Modern Tools

- Experiment with relationship-focused apps like **Paired, Lasting,** or **Woebot**.

- Set boundaries for technology use, such as "tech-free zones" during meals or bedtime.
- Reflect regularly on whether your use of technology enhances or hinders your connection.

Future-Proofing Your Relationship

- Embrace change by exploring innovative tools, like virtual date nights or AI-driven insights.
- Stay grounded by prioritizing analog traditions, like handwritten notes or spontaneous gestures.
- Revisit your shared values and goals regularly to ensure alignment.

An Invitation to Thrive

At its core, this book isn't just about tools or techniques—it's about transformation. It's about becoming the kind of partner who listens deeply, communicates authentically, and navigates challenges with grace. It's about building a relationship that not only survives but thrives, grounded in mutual respect, trust, and connection.

As you move forward, here are three guiding principles to keep at the heart of your journey:

1. **Stay Curious:** Relationships are dynamic. Keep learning about yourself, your partner, and the evolving tools that can support your growth.

Curiosity is the key to staying connected and engaged.

2. **Lead with Empathy:** Approach every interaction with understanding and compassion. When conflicts arise, remind yourself that you're on the same team, working toward the same goals.

3. **Celebrate Progress:** Perfection isn't the goal—progress is. Every small step you take toward smarter love is a victory worth celebrating.

Your Next Steps

1. Reflect on the strategies that resonated most with you. Choose one to implement this week.
2. Share your intentions with your partner, inviting them to join you on this journey of growth.
3. Revisit this book regularly, using it as a resource to guide your relationship through new challenges and opportunities.

Final Thoughts

Smart love is more than a concept—it's a practice. It's the small, consistent choices you make every day to show up fully for yourself and your partner. With the tools and insights shared in this book, you're equipped to build a relationship that thrives on clarity, trust, and intentional connection.

Remember, love isn't static—it's a journey. And with each step, you have the opportunity to grow smarter, stronger, and closer together. So, take a deep breath, reflect on what you've learned, and step forward with confidence. The future of your love life is bright, and it starts with the actions you take today.

Go forth and build a relationship that reflects the best of both your humanity and the tools that support it. Because smart love isn't just about having the right strategies—it's about creating a life of connection, growth, and enduring joy.

www.ingramcontent.com/pod-product-compliance
Lightning Source LLC
Chambersburg PA
CBHW061641250726
48659CB00004B/1333